NEVER AGAIN

1994/95
A SEASON
IN THE
RED ZONE

A RED FINAL PUBLICATION

ISBN 0 952697 0 0 9

Published by The Red Final, PO Box 368, Aberdeen, AB9 8AE

Typeset & Edited by Uncle Albert, assisted by The Count and OBE, who all apologise now for any errors they might have missed.

The Ancient Greek philosophers called it catharsis, the need to emit the primal scream in order to exorcise the pain within and to help in the search for the true meaning and value of life. In modern society, right wing politicians and leaders justify their attacks on the living standards of their people by uttering the Thatcherite maxim, "No gain without pain".

In the season just gone by, no Aberdeen supporter ever talked to me about catharsis. I heard no-one trot out the sad, reactionary one-liner beloved of free marketeers. Small wonder.

There is no such thing as a divine right to success in football, despite what the press and TV wish on behalf of their Ibrox darlings. Over the years, as Aberdeen supporters, we have become used to success, although this has been less in evidence in recent years. Nevertheless, we do not deserve to have been put through the emotional mincer as we were in season 1994/95.

A mark of quality, as all good management texts tell us, is the willingness and ability to learn from mistakes. These have been made in all areas of the club and have led to the seemingly sudden decline into the depths that constituted 1994/95. Organisations that fail or enter a spiral of decline are not subject to sudden changes in circumstances. Business is gradually eroded away. When was the earliest writing on the wall seen? And anyway, does this matter?

We must learn from the crisis that engulfed all stakeholders in AFC during the torrid months of 1994/95, but we must neither dwell on this nor look for scapegoats. Such recrimination will only seek to divert all of us from doing our utmost to take the fight to the enemy in their ain middens. The final weeks of the season proved what could be achieved if all with the future of the club at heart pulled in the same direction with constancy of purpose.

This slim volume has been written to exorcise some of the pain and to relive what little joy there was during the blackest period in living memory, when the jaws of the First Division snapped, but with Dundee United in their grip rather than us.

It is dedicated to the supporters of Aberdeen who, defying popular myth about our lack of feeling, kicked butt and rallied round the flag to passionately declare the importance of our club to the whole community. You were, and are, magnificent.

Come On You Reds!

What follows is not a blow by blow account of season 94/95, but a collection of essays reminiscing the few highs and copious lows of last year.

It is dedicated to every Dons' fan who suffered the slings and arrows of outrageous performances during the season to become the inspiration behind the scramble to safety.

Stories, characters and incidents mentioned in the book are entirely factual, probably.

Keep the faith

Sparky

CONTENTS

All Illustrations by Gordon Reid

A Room With a View

A foreword by John McRuvie

Lately, during rare moments of peace and quiet in the McRuvie household (bairn sleeping, wife bathing, telly nothing), my thoughts turn to my rookie year as AFC's Matchday announcer.

As you are all well aware, Aberdeen's 94/95 season had too few 'ups' and one 'nearly going down'. To quote Les Dawson, "We've 'ad more lows than a Japanese phone book". However, don't expect me to start telling you what went wrong last season as I haven't a clue where to start looking. Although I love my footie, I am neither expert nor analyst. The clues are there but for me to find them would require the assistance of Scooby Doo and his gang. (Apparently Scooby lays the blame on Smiffy who would have got away with it had he not been sacked due to those meddling kids.) The why him, the how long, the Will-ie, the what ifs and the who are they, who are they, who are they, I will leave to the writers of the excellent book you are about to read because, as you will soon discover, 'The Red Final' does it better than anyone.

Although the season past is one that will be remembered as 'The Great Escape', I must admit that I enjoyed every minute of it. I know what you're thinking; did I watch the same home matches as you did? Chic Young would have cause to bleat, "Were you at the game?" However, the low points that we all suffered have been greatly outnumbered by the high points that I have personally experienced. From the moment I said yes, yes and thrice yes when first offered the position, right up until Stephen Glass waltzed in our sixth goal at East End Park, and beyond (as you will discover later), my own 'season' has had its moments.

For instance, when I asked you to applaud the return of Alex McLeish as manager of Motherwell and you granted Big Red a standing ovation, to which he replied with a 3-1 thumping. Or Chic Charnley's sad attempts at striking Angus the Costume with a football when I replied that he "couldn't hit that bull's arse with a banjo". I must have got his dander up because the bampot scored the equaliser. Then there was the match when I broadcast: "Erra substitution forra Cellick, number twelve Donnelly by the way". After the match I heard a Tim in a blazer telling one of our blazers, "Yer DJ's a wee but biased is he no!!" I will also never forget the Dunfermline supporter who continued his team's post first leg greetin theme in a letter claiming that the "Pittodrie announcer took as much time to read the entire Dunfermline team as he did to say, 'NUMBER ONE, THEO SNELDERS' ". "Happy to have pissed you off even more sir," would have been the short reply had the numpty sent his address. The reason for this unbridled form of prepossessed broadcasting by your matchday announcer can all be explained in one statement: "THIS IS OUR HOUSE." Enough said.

There were other moments this season that enabled me to view the sporting media from inside the looking glass. I stood next to Bill Leckie (and don't you forget it) in the Falkirk press box as he and his fellow hun-loving hack, Ewan Graham, annoyed that they had to stand because the Northsound team had taken over their seats, and pissed off at the 2-0 scoreline, cheered up no end when the news filtered through from Tynecastle that Big Eck and his Steelmen were not 'Backing the Dons'. Smiles, high fives and shaking of fists followed behind the Northsound commentary team. I passed a note to Andrew Shinie with the word 'Wanker' written in bold print. He passed it back after writing the word 'Fucking' above it. Great gags never die. No sooner had our hooligans in suits calmed down, than from about five or six rows below us a Dandy stood up screaming for a free kick. (John Clark had just clattered his umpteenth opponent.) Nothing bad in that (I speak of the Dandy not the Donkey). Certainly nothing compared to the huns ripping out seats after penalties were denied to them at Pittodrie last season, also witnessed from the gantry. SCUM!! Our brave Dandy was soon ordered to sit down by the Falkirk mob that surrounded him. Certainly not the mob surrounding the Northsound sports team, namely Bill Leckie (and don't you regret him) or Ewan Graham as they reported throughout the week in the "ranger". Look out for Ewan Graham as the next Roger de Courcey with Bill Leckie as Nookie the teddy bear (and don't you feed him). When they did finally sit down at the end of the match, I thought their voices became rather muffled, which would lay proof to the Red Final's argument that these two hun-sucking parasites talk out of their arses.

Another media incident took place on the day we gave the huns a February Sunday stuffing. I was sitting in the gantry, broad-casting the teams, when the door opened and in walked a televi-sion producer, or tea boy, or both, due to the cutbacks. Anyway, he interrupts me in full swing, "Number One Theo Snel....". He then asks me if the reason for one end of the ground being full of kids was due to the fact that there was a 'special freebie' on that day, because in his words, "The commentator needs to know". Yes, that's right. He needs to know because he needs to tell the nation. Our first match since the departure of our greatest player, the threat of defeat, our league position at the time and if that wasn't enough bad news for him to broadcast to the couch potatoes of the iprix loyal, our unbiased commentator also wanted to announce how many kids got in for free.

It was made all the more bizarre by the fact that the last time the telly circus appeared at Pittodrie, the same guy had asked me exactly the same question. I've always wondered which part of the title 'Merkland Family Stand' written on the structure in foot high letters, he found hard to understand. Next time he pays a call to the gantry (first hun visit I suspect) I'm going to interrupt him by asking a stupid question that I already know the answer to. "Why do you point all your field microphones in the direction of the east wing of the South Stand??" Yes folks, the West Coast media is alive and kicking at its partisan best and don't ever be fooled by those who tell you that there is no such thing as coloured broad-casting or journalism in Scottish Football.

When I look back over last season's jukebox of memories, there are four which stand out from the rest like a blind cobbler's thumb. In true DJ fashion I will recall them in reverse order of greatness. What else would you expect?

Number Four........

Neil McDougall, the then president of the Association of Aberdeen Supporters Clubs, invited Donna and I to their annual dinner. That evening, we were placed at the top table next to the then manager of AFC, Willie Miller, and for the best part of an hour, I talked, but mainly listened to my all time hero. His speech that evening focused on his never ending thirst for success, his love for the club and his desire to stick it right up the River Clyde. No written speech, just straight from where it mattered. The invited AFC director, who, as he put it, had "drawn the short straw", babbled through what felt like a six page, A3-size essay written by oriental miniature craftsmen. Willie's speech was fifty percent longer and a zillion percent superior. The man is immense. In the top ten list of my all time AFC moments, this one, like the Willie I want to remember, will never pass number six.

Number Three........

The Goalmeister, His Majesty the King Shearer of Duncan and last season's many Winter Wonderlands we walked along, singing a song. His first timer against the Arabs was more breathtaking than the move leading up to it. His 87th minute goal against the huns to put us 2-0 ahead back in February. I almost fell out of the window with excitement. I cannot explain to you how I feel during the thirty seconds between a Shearer strike and my broadcast of the goal. All I can say is that my voice trembles and I sweat like a Turk in a snorkel parka. If the man ever scores a double hat-trick at Pittodrie against the huns, I'll end up thinner than a paperboy's wage packet. The best moment is the scene around the ground following my "Goal for Aberdeen" announcement. The cheer followed by the singing of his anthem is a sight and sound that's second to none. My favourite of his was our third against the moaning Pars. Who better to give us the last home goal of season 94/95? One touch after beating the offside trap

10

(from my view by at least a yard), one look up at the goal and bingo, Hallelujah and Bob's your auntie's live-in lover.

Three-One; "It's a goal D-U-N-C-A-N S-H-E-A-R-E-R!!!"

Number Two.........

I was leaving the ground after we beat the Arabs to move off the bottom of the table (phew). Roy Aitken was trackside with the BBC waiting to go live to the country. As I passed he moved to one side, congratulated me on a job well done, patted me on the back and ordered me to go to Brockville the following week and hijack the announcer. He then jumped back in front of the camera and continued to wait until the studio (w)anchorman Dougie Donnelly had finished talking about the old firm. At that moment if Roy had said to me, "Shit", I would have crouched down and replied, "What colour do you want it?". Driving home that evening I kept hearing Prince in my head singing, "I would die for U" over and over again. This moment was made all the sweeter because my father, the man who once lifted me over the barrier to get Davie Robb's autograph many moons ago, was there to witness it. Three months on and he is still telling this story to anyone with a pair of ears and an empty glass.

That weekend I floated out of Pittodrie ten feet in the air. The following week I was at Brockville standing six feet from the announcer and six inches from Ewan Graham and Bill Leckie (and don't you detest him). History will show that I was not required to carry out my duty for the cause, but by Christ was I prepared. Thank you Roy. The sooner every Dandy meets you, the better.

And Now - This year's Number ONE........

It happened on Friday, June 2, 1995, eight days into our close season and miles from Pittodrie. I was invited, along with my Northsound ally and friend, the vertically-challenged Thistle fan Dave Macdermid, to attend an end of season dinner at the Craighaar Hotel, hosted by those mortals who write, draw, publish and retail the AFC fanzine, 'The Red Final'. Having been an ardent reader

11

since Volume 0 Issue 0, you can imagine I was once again a fan among heroes. That evening, I was given the honour of placing faces to such mythical names as The Count, Bloo Toon, Sparky, OBE, Mainly Standing, Uncle Albert, Gordon Reid and Niall. During the meal, I cheered when they produced a photo of an ex-postie and burnt it at the stake (pie). During the coffee I joined in the singing of The Red Final's favourite songs, *"All Around My Hat"*, *"Somebody Stole My Sombrero"* and *"Who Ate All The Pies?"*. During the speeches, I laughed constantly at the anecdotes which flowed as often and as rich as the wine. To cap a splendid evening we made our way to the Paramount Bar where I joined the lads for a Red Final Gobathon at the video-bog. The scene that followed the arrival on screen of B. O. Hateley (the world's favourite (h)airline) has been locked away in a time capsule for a thousand years. Without doubt, this was THE number one event for me last season.

What can I tell you about these men? Well on the outside they look just like you, me, or almost anyone else for that matter. Noticed how I wrote "almost anyone else"? This is because thankfully none of them look like Jim Traynor. However, it's the inside that counts. During conversations with them you can sense a true love and respect for their club. There are occasions when the pride they show sticks out like a T-shirt clad Dolly Parton atop the Broad Hill in February. They are all genuine, die-hard, rain or shine, Neighbours then Home and Away, season ticket-holding supporters of the Dons. Their knowledge of AFC's history is amazing. The teams of the day, the scorer of the goal, the tally of the crowd, the direction of the wind, the temperature of the pies and the weakness of the bovril are so well recalled that if you close your eyes you're there. Once, during a sixties revival directed by The Count, I started singing "Ai-ber-deen, cha, cha, cha". It was spooky. Yes folks, contrary to the propaganda written over the years by the local press and an ex-postie, The Red Final shoots from the hip and writes from the heart in a style that fellow scribes wish they had written. One in particular takes the easy route by attempting to jump on their bandwagon. Don't believe me? Look at the number of column inches written by His Royal Girthness, Charlie Allan, dedicated to the pie-eating story in issue number twelve of TRF. Don't let him jump on board your success-wagon boys, he'll only burst the bloody tyres.

Let's make no bones about it, the administrators of The Red

Final are fans and I don't mean the half way down King Street at ten past three during a home match fan, nor the fan who travels to an away match because the hospitality is free and plentiful (hang on, that's the same fan!). That is not the way with the men of The Red Final. They are honest, genuine, hard-earned cash spending fans of Aberdeen Football Club, long before they sit down in front of their computers and type their columns. That's the bottom line and it speaks volumes. Just like the book you are about to enjoy.

Looking forward to next season, I only hope and pray that the mistakes made in 94/95 have been discovered, rectified and are never allowed to happen again. We must make sure that the grim reaper of Division One is never allowed to travel as far north as he did last season when he got to the Duthie Park roundabout before turning back to Jute City.

What surprises are in store for us next season?? Silverware at the end perhaps?? No one can tell, but some things are certain. You the fans will continue to give 100% backing to the team, just as you did during last season's good times and even more so in the bad. But even more special will be the fact that next season The Red Final will continue to acknowledge the brave, cut down the weak and tell it like it is.

John McRuvie (The native Kincorther)

Sten Guns Over Kincardine Bridge ....18 February 1995

My first recollection of hearing that Stenhousemuir were still in the Scottish Cup was when I heard that we had been drawn away to them or St. Johnstone in Round Four. Aren't they always knocked out early catflaps by Deveronvale or Third Division newcomers Inverness Thistle before the Premier Prima Donnas deign to grace the tournament?

"Oh no," I thought, "Not St. Johnstone again", remembering

the hard time they had given us last season. Even when Saints lost an equaliser very late letterboxes, my assumption was that they would still be too strong for one of Scotland's joke teams in the replay.

BBC Scotland News announced, "4-0 Stenhousemuir". Three thoughts: (a) the BBC have got this the wrong way round. Nope. Never happens. This is the last refuge of the eternally optimistic; Kilmarnock 3 Aberdeen 1 is reality, my friend. (b) thank Christ we've avoided St. Johnstone, but they must be shite to have lost to that lot. (c) Mad Mac (oh come on now, you know he's the editor of 'The Absolute Game', have you not been paying attention?), Saints addict, will be suicidal.

Trauma followed trauma for me during that period. We'd struggled to remove Stranraer in the Third Round at Pittodrie, Kilmarnock had beaten us comprehensively at Rugby Park and for the first time I contemplated relegation as a probability, Wull exited bejottered by the Board, Sir Royston of Aitkenburgh took over, my life entered another year and in a day of intense emotion we stuffed the Huns at home. One word thoughts on the above, chronologically expressed? Phew. Disbelief. Gutted. Why? Resignation. Orgasmic.

Had the corner been turned? Had the bloody corner even been awarded? All the rumours about The Former (Retired Undefeated) Best Penalty Box Defender In The World having lost the respect of the players began to look as though they might have contained a smidginlet of truth. Why did they turn it on for Roy and not for TF(RU)BPBDITW?

Let me say at this point that I have never subscribed to the theory that players try their hardest only as and when they feel like it. Christ, it's bad enough being on the losing side when you play in Seaton Park on Tuesday evenings in Summer with jacket goals, and nothing at stake other than the desire to win the game. Up the stakes slightly and play for a Welfare or Amateur side and defeat can ruin the entire week. Incidentally, the term 'welfare' is a definite misnomer - whenever did you hear of 'welfare' being anything to do with the game as it's played at that level? Even when football is your livelihood, the basic winning instinct must still exist before win bonuses are even considered. Then there's the mortgage to pay, the bookie to keep in business and the harem of leggy blonde bimbos to buy expensive cocktails for in

Cafe Society on a Saturday night. I'll listen to any arguments to the contrary if the players under discussion include Jim Bett, Billy Stark or Robert Connor though.....

The build-up to the Stenny match took a predictable course. All week, the players were being quoted, the manager (caretaker) was opining that our opponents were not to be taken lightly, and the Directors had even raised their heads above the parapet to talk of the need to involve the supporters more, issue shares, become a community club...blah...blah...blah.

There was talk of us being only 360 minutes from lifting the trophy......relegation pressure being lifted......new team spirit after skelping the Huns' collective erse.....the Cup a chance to shine away from the fight in the Premier cellar......a place in Europe via the ECWC and general optimism that the bad times were behind us. As long-suffering Aberdeen fans, we should know by this time that one swallow does not make a summer. Nor does one swallow make a post-match drinking session.

As OBE, Mainly Standing and your author careered towards Kinross Services for the now traditional slash break and mental preparation for the assault on Hun heartland which lies immediately on the other side of the Kincardine Bridge, the mood in the Finalmobile was as cheery as it ever can get when Curmudgeons Anonymous have an in-car therapy session. I confess to having had a mental picture of us going a goal down with 15 minutes to go, and wondering what our heroes' reaction would be to such a nightmare scenario. Dismissal of such negativity was called for. This was Stenhousemuir, after all, not one of the giants to whom we had fallen e.g. Airdrie, Kilmarnock, Motherwell. Secretly, despite the previous Sunday's result against the Huns, I would have settled for a draw and fancied our chances in a second game. Go on, admit it, so would you. Aye, aye, *now*, but then?

Stenhousemuir itself was in exactly the mood that small towns with Cup fever usually are. False bravado and forced optimism were much in evidence. Most fans were wearing brand new scarves and you can bet that among the throng heading for their date with destiny were those whose allegiances lay thirty miles to the west. You know where I mean. Once-a-season inquisitive airheads who would recognise all of our players and none of "their own". The real parasites of the game, unwanted and despised by those who are regular supporters of both sides. I only hope that

16

the very youngest of the new fans that day make going to support their local club a regular Saturday activity. No doubt, as usual, peer pressure and not a little intimidation and violence will dictate.

Ochilview is a tip. No surprise there. Our lot dutifully filtered in behind one goal and raised a fair racket and the players during the warm-up seemed very pleased to see such a healthy support in town. This health was quantifiable in numbers only - vast quantities of alcohol had been bellied and dodgy pies were oozing lukewarm grease down a thousand arms. Remember the old Health Promotions slogan? Fit fans don't abuse booze. On a point of pure punctuation, I always considered that the statement should have ended with a question mark. And I would have been unable to provide an answer.

Well, what a bloody way to repay such loyalty and solidarity. From very early on, it was clear that we did not have the bottle for the battle that it was becoming. Eoin Jess (footballer), who had delighted us by scampering through the Hun defence only six days before, was at the Ochilview fancy dress party wearing his favourite 'enigma' costume. Billy Dodds was out of touch, McKimmie out of his depth, Joe Miller out of luck with a close-range header and by the thirty minute mark, most of us were out of our minds with worry as Miller Mathieson, Tommy Steele and the slaphead goalie unpacked the spray cans and began to put the writing on the wall.

By half time I had decided that a draw would be a good result. The defence was looking rocky - perhaps Sylvester Stallone, goalkeeping star of crap film "Escape To Victory" should have been transferred in - and Theo, Smithy and Inglis had almost had a stand-up scrap after one particular louse-up.

Where was the midfield? Playing for bloody Oldham, that's where. Why Rico, why? Waddell, Smith, McCluskey, Thow, Mottram....that's why. Need we go further?

As the second half progressed the inevitable was sensed by a large part of the crowd, both ours and theirs. We were being hemmed in to our own half by a team of milkmen, bakers and message boys. Occasional forays into their half led to nothing. We carried no threat and any confidence taken from the win against the Huns had long since disappeared. A scramble in our penalty area led to the ball not being cleared (was it John Greig who used to say "oot o' the park for medals"?) and Tommy Steele, whose name was a godsend to all crap headline writers, took his time, steadied himself, combed his quiff, yawned, gave his sphincter a lazy scratch and only then decided to fire the ball behind our defence and swing the pendulum firmly in Stenhousemuir's direction.

Cue mutterings of protest from the Sheepshagging element, and vain attempts to raise flagging spirits by growling some anthems of support. We knew it wasn't worth the effort - shite and we're going out. A brief flurry around the Stenhousemuir goal that was ably dealt with provided only brief respite from the doing we were getting. And then the part-timers scored again. A corner from the left, a hole the size of a family size very big thing appeared in the middle of our penalty box, and up popped udder-handler Lord Thomas Steele of the Byre to volley the ball home.

The home crowd were now going completely monkey turds. Our players were so demoralised that they forgot to argue with each other about who was to blame. The Dons' end emptied as the realisation dawned. We had been done HL and S by a Second Division horde who would have been treated with contempt two years ago. I felt lower than an adder's scrotum.

Those who had chosen to leave the ground left behind dozens who hovered around the incongruous looking stand. They sang about Willie Miller, they chanted for the Board to be sacked, they howled for the heads of some of the players. All actions were a waste of time. Willie was long gone, and if rumours are right, his indignant wife Claire was dancing around the Parkway pool table in delight when she heard the score coming through from Ochilview. Silly woman, allegedly. The Board is the employer at Pittodrie, and would find it difficult to sack themselves. I mean, who would employ the next lot? As for calling for the players' heads, this was futile. Some of them had their heads missing (as in chickens), and others were so far up their own arses that they would have been impossible to find.

The protesters had my admiration until the final whistle when Charlie Allan of the 'Evening Express' left the stand. Several (i.e. seven or eight and not the three or four hundred he claimed) rushed towards him. Despite our antipathy towards Sir Turgid of Prose we did not want to see him being attacked by a mob. Not to worry. The most bizarre thing I saw all season happened. They started to

18

shake his hand. His worried look changed to relief as he, the sav-
iour of the Dons, agreed with their point of view and waddled pur-
posefully off to write a suitably condemnatory piece about how the
club had gone to rack, and in all fairness, ruin. Short short memories. Allan had been one of the main perpetrators of the myth that
we were going through a temporary bad patch and had been the
main apologist for the club for years, failing to spot the rot at the
core. Too late, he voiced the opinions of those who could see what
was really happening. Come the revolution though, tovarich...........

The Stenhousemuir fanzine "The Duffle", in celebrating the cup
run, paid tribute to the reactions of the Aberdeen fans who remained in their places at the final whistle.

*"In a sporting gesture a large section of the Dons fans also
applauded our team as they left the park, which renewed my faith
in most football supporters as being decent folk."*

"The Duffle", Issue 9. April 1995. Page 14.
(We await reconsideration of this last statement should the
Huns ever visit Ochilview.....)

*"Credit here to the remaining Dons supporters behind the goal
who joined in the round of applause for the victorious home team.
That was sportsmanship in its finest form. Let's face it, they must
have been shattered. Well done folks, you deserve a more successful team to watch!"*

*"...The cheering locals mingled with distraught and silent Ab-
erdeen fans in Tryst Road with no hint of trouble. Again great
credit to the visitors for this."*

Ibid. Page 23.

Shades of Skonto Riga earlier in the season. Why not? They
deserved it....it'll never catch on if we ever again lose to the Huns
though.

Before we left the ground, I met Hamish, an acquaintance
who now has a Pittodrie Season Ticket, but whose roots and heart
lie in Larbert. On congratulating him as graciously as I could, he
introduced me to his father, a lifelong Stenny fan and share-
holder, who, nearly in tears, announced that this was the fulfil-
ment of his dreams. This elderly man made the most cutting and

sensible comment of the day when he said, "There's two divisions between those teams, and you couldn't tell the difference today." Yes, Hamish's dad, hole in one. We were that bad.

We could see no way back from the depths we had reached. Nothing left to play for but the scrap against the drop. Being patronised by jubilant, disbelieving fans of a team who should not have been able to live with us. To have seen at first hand the performance was bad enough. To have listened to the whooping and hollering on the airwaves of Scotland's broadcasting media must have been worse. Anyone whose only access to the developments was via Teletext could only have assumed that Alex Cameron or Jim Traynor had bound and gagged the guy who normally did the typing, locked him in the Ceefax lobby press and gleefully operated a sinister Ministry of Misinformation beaming into telescreens all over Europe. Elsewhere in this volume, Nervus Brocher gives his account of what it was like to watch the season-long demise far from the scene. And how did Sparky, in London on some EE-sponsored second honeymoon with Mrs. Sparky (and if it wasn't with Mrs. Sparky, I'm sorry old pal, I've dropped you in it) find out? At least back in driech Larbert, we had each other to whom we could mutter grunts of disbelief.

As always with tragic events, realisation does not sink in until well after the coup de grace has been administered and by the time coffee and sticky buns were being taken at Kinross, and Mainly was "smoking snouts like Virginia was in flames", the severity of the situation had begun to dawn on us. It was a quiet journey, but every cloud, as Mr. Cliche once said, has a silvery lining and OBE's car radio was bust. No "Off The Ball", therefore. Splice the mainbrace, and double rations to each man.

At home, the house cold and unwelcoming since Mrs. Count and the Countlettes were on some 'stay-in-the-will' parental visit, "The Green Final" lay in wait on the mat like a particularly green papery thing with revenge in mind for the bad-mouthing it gets from me each Saturday. Charlie's witterings about "the most humiliating result in the club's proud 92 year history" were bad enough, but it got worse. "Sportscene", later on had Dougie Donnelly chortling and Lardbucket Johnstone gloating as they interviewed Stenny's chairman, decked out in club blazer and spanking new scarf. I could have cried. Yvonne Fair once soulfully wailed, "It should have been me". I knew just how she felt.

This whole turgid season has been one for avoiding the Sunday papers. Sunday 19th February was typical and then some. Then there was work to face on Monday morning. The guys from the City Bar Reds, who stated in the 'EE' that the worst backstabbers in the game are those who make their living in the North East and who take pleasure in badmouthing the Dons at every turn, got it spot on. They seem to take delight in downturns in our fortunes. Yet, these are the same gloryhunting tossers who badger us for tickets whenever there's a bandwagon ready to leave for Successville. I take no pleasure from giving the true fans of other teams a hard time. My Arab acquaintances, for example, have had no gloating calls or faxes from me since our win over them or their drop into Division One. I can imagine myself in their position. I know that their support for their side is in most cases as fanatical as mine is for the past, current and future crops of the Merkland Misfits. Only too well do I remember being the only Red at a country town primary school and taking crap from brainless Huns and Tims who had never even seen their chosen ones play. Pinning colour posters on bedroom walls does not a football supporter make. Help! Nearly slipped into Jack Webster When-I-Was-A-Country-Loon-Mode there.

So, out of the Cup, floundering in the brown stuff in the lavvy pan of that toilet that is the Premier Division. Pass the 12-bore, mother, I've got an urgent appointment with a Mr. G. Reaper behind the steading.

Could there possibly be a way back? At that point in time, it seemed very, very unlikely.

Surely our worst ever day.

21

All Aboard The Emotional Roller-Coaster

It began on a sunny day in Aberdeen in August and ended with that same sun shining down on a patch of green grass in Dunfermline late on a May evening. In between, followers of Aberdeen FC had little black clouds following them around morning, noon and night. There were sporadic breaks in this cloud, but for the most part, the blackness prevailed.

Saddam Hussein - were he a Dons fan (although he's probably a Hun) - would probably have called it "the mother of all seasons". To me it was more like "the mother-in-law of all seasons".

For some strange reason, when we got together to decide to write this little masterpiece, I was the one who promptly volunteered to talk about what this season had done to, and with, our emotions. At that time - after the play-off first leg - I think all our emotions had taken a pretty severe battering, and it seemed a fairly easy topic to write about.

That was six weeks ago. And as the dust has now settled on that miserable, barren season, and we look forward - as only football fans can do - with renewed optimism to the season ahead, the roller-coaster ride our emotions have just been on seems a little distant.

A roller-coaster it most certainly was, for just when we'd suffered a couple of bad defeats we'd get a win and think, "right that's us back on track again", only to lose again the next Saturday. That happened several times during season 94/95, and towards the end we all realised that we couldn't depend on us turning any corners on the basis of one win - we were simply too bad to be able to rely on that sort of logic.

The season was sprinkled liberally with incidents which, for one reason or another, had us all searching for a high building, from which we could either proclaim our side's greatness, or, alternatively, take a flier. For what it's worth, I'm going to vent my spleen over what it's been like for me to follow the Dons in season 94/95. Hopefully, what you're about to read will bring back the emotional highlights and low lights for you as well.

Here they are then - the emotions...

Anger

I'm going to start with our captain, and why not? You see at the end of that first game in August, I came out onto Golf Road waxing lyrical about McKimmie's display. He played like a captain that day. The fact that it was his fault we lost a goal against Hearts seemed irrelevant - as I looked forward to McKimmie finally stamping his authority on the side.

Little did I know that later on in the season, he would be very nearly stamping his size 8 boot over a Dons' fan in the Main Stand.

Part-way through the season, with a few bad results under our belt and just when we were all getting a bit concerned over what the season held for us, McKimmie was the guy who took all the flak. Most teams have a fall-guy and for a large part of the season McKimmie was that man.

The fans looked for a target and aimed their anger towards him. I have to admit that an expression of hatred was never far from my lips any time McKimmie was mentioned. My animosity towards this local loon had many facets. Firstly, his form was very poor. The weakest part of his game - his passing - seemed to have sunk to new lows. Each pass that went astray was met with derision from the terraces, and me in particular.

It got to the point that as he was about to pass the ball, this little guy in my head said, "Go on McKimmie screw it up so that I can slag ye off ye useless bastard". Not a healthy state for a 'fan' to be in.

Also in relation to his form, many goals that were lost (certainly up to mid-season) were quite obviously McKimmie's fault. In addition, he made many defensive errors during the season which potentially could have led to an increase in the "goals against" column. At the end of the day Jock, the boy just wasn't playing well.

Next on the McKimmie hit list was the fact that he was our captain. He had the misfortune of following guys like Miller and McLeish into the captain's role, and to be fair it was never going to be easy for anyone to pull on the armband after those two. He was accused by many of not being able to motivate the team. He never shouted at his team-mates. No inspiration or organisation came from McKimmie. He was probably a nice lad, but not a leader. Even the Joe Harpers and Derek Johnstones of the world were openly saying that we had no leader on the park.

"Probably a nice lad" - yeah. Try telling that to the fans he's hurled abuse at from the pitch. As soon as he started this nonsense, many hundreds of fans turned on him, and although most never voiced this inside the ground, there was an underlying current of anger towards him.

The local evening paper didn't help matters by printing stories about how McKimmie and the team in general, were happier to play away from Pittodrie because away fans gave the team su-

perb backing - hinting that home fans were a waste of space. Maybe
we shouldn't have bothered turning up for the next home game -
wonder how Mrs. McKimmie would have coped in Asda with only a
couple of quid to spend. He also said that the team played better
away from home and were more likely to win. Cue the ensuing run
of away defeats...

Throughout all these troubled times for McKimmie and the
side, Willie was intent on playing him game after game. If he had
been playing poorly but fulfilling the captain's role, as his manager once did, then we could certainly have forgiven him.

It has to be said that he came good in the end, for as we approached the critical last few games of the season, McKimmie
played like the player we knew he could be. Unfortunately, I
believe some supporters (myself included) will never really be
able to forgive him for those battles with the fans.

Fear

Many of us departed Pittodrie sporting the proverbial brown-
stained underpants on several occasions last season. The fear was,
quite simply, of our being relegated for the first time in our history.
I guess for me the fear really set in when Killie beat us at Pittodrie
- on April 1st of all days. This was the fourth time we had lost to
them, and represented the first time a club has done a white-
wash on us - four wins out of four in the Premier League. Firmly
anchored at the bottom of the league, our fate seemed sealed.

The fear factor weighed even more on our already heavily
burdened shoulders as defeats at Ibrox and Fir Park meant that
climbing up the league table would be a bit like Stevie Wonder
climbing Everest solo, with Wolf from the Gladiators hitting him
all the way up with one of those big stick things.

During those bleak days, the fear of life in Division One began to become apparent. Most of the Scottish sporting hacks were
gleefully reminding us just how much it would cost the club to go
down a division and falling over themselves to proclaim that our
best players wouldn't want to stay with a First Division club.
We were worried, not so much by the stuff in the press, but more
because we knew in our hearts that the club looked doomed.

25

I remember coming home from that Killie game and not being able to think about anything else the rest of the evening. My usual routine coming home from a game is that for the first hour I'm back in the house I'll relive all the important bits of the game in my mind, and maybe try to relate some of them to the young lad. That night was different. I was scared. I was so scared that I almost picked up the phone to call Ricky Simpson. The club meant so much to me that I was actually going to phone this guy up and ask him and his mate Rod to buy Ian Donald out.

Apart from being afraid of relegation itself, there were other longer term horrors which faced us, like; "What if we went down there and never got back up again?" Would we become just like the Dundees and Dunfermlines of this world - destined forever more to live on the fringes of top flight Scottish soccer? Worse still - would we end up like Morton or Clyde? Sounds incredible now, but six months ago these fears were real.

What about the Board? We began to fear (once again) that they really didn't give a shit. The club was on a one-way trip into footballing oblivion and they were doing nothing about it. Some will tell you that the board were also scared, and this then manifested itself in the panic sacking of Willie. But that I will grant you is arguable.

And the players - let's not forget them in all this - their livelihoods were at stake and the way some of our *star* names were performing made sure there wouldn't be a lengthy queue of scouts and agents at their doors come the end of the season.

In truth, we all probably suffered the fear factor to some extent.

Ecstasy

Several nominations for this category surprisingly enough. How about these...

1. Scott Booth's goal against the Huns on Sept. 24th.

A long ball came through towards Booth who had Boli shadowing him. Booth managed to shrug the lumbering catholic off before unleashing an un-stoppable shot past little fat turd Goram. YYYYYYYYYEEEEEEEEEEEEEEEESSSSSSSSSSS.

2. Duncan Shearer's second goal against the Huns at Ibrox on April 8th.

We had gone 2-0 down and just been beaten by Killie at home the previous Saturday. Luckily for me I wasn't there and instead was at home listening to the radio as I was doing some decorating. Dodds pulled one back and we were back in the game. My nerves couldn't take it so I decided to go downstairs and get a drink from the kitchen. I couldn't resist switching on the portable TV and getting updates on the teletext. Multiple orgasm time as I find out that Shearer has equalised. I yell out a YEEEEEEEEEESSSSSSSSS at max. volume, spot an empty cardboard box on the floor and start kicking the shit out of it. For my piece de resistance, I start singing at top volume "It's a goal Duncan Shearer" to my kitchen wall hoping that the neighbours on the other side of the wall will hear it - he's a Hun who wears "5 in a row" T-shirts - you know the type.

3. Billy Dodds' winning goal against Hearts at Tynecastle on April 28th.

We simply had to win this game and did, courtesy of Billy's nod-ded winner in the 89th minute. Unbelievable scenes of joy followed. The section of the Main Stand we were in that day must have come close to collapsing as me and several hundred other Dandies went crazy.

More Hugh Grant type ecstasy was to follow as news came through that Hibs had gone 1-0 up against Dundee Utd. I remember looking across to the end most of the Dandies occupied and they were going completely mental - a sight I'll never forget.

We made our way deliriously happy from the Edinburgh slum that day, goading Hearts fans as we came out (they were still in danger of the drop at that time). As we headed out of the city in the car, we found ourselves behind a lone Dandy in a dark blue Ford Escort. We exchanged pleasantries by way of our horns until we parted company just before the city bypass. Sparky and my mate continued to scream "2-1 to the Aberdeen" out of the windows at any Edinburgh citizen that we passed by. I do seem to remember also that the car roof took a fair dunting from us so that we could have a percussion backing to the haunting melody.

4. Shearer's second goal v Dunfermline in the first leg of the play-offs.

As I normally do with a Shearer goal, my head turned to the skies (yet I only saw the stand roof) and proclaimed the man's greatness. Do you think players like him realise what they do to us when they score a goal? The way he latched on to the through ball from Irvine, controlled it with his left and BLASTED it with his right was something more outrageously orgasmic than anything I've ever seen. He truly is THE man.

For a moment every single cell in my body was consumed with sheer ecstasy. In addition to the way he took the goal, it meant that we were hanging onto Premier survival with a firm grip and starting to pull ourselves up.

Despair

It was just so miserable wasn't it? Coming away from Pittodrie after another defeat and heading into the cold and rain. Not much point in talking about the game - what could you say - another defeat. It got to the stage where you couldn't even pin it on the referee. We were crap and we knew it. Did you manage to lift your spirits much off ground level as you headed home in your supporters' bus or in your car?

There was no light at the end of the tunnel was there? Skonto Riga, Stenhousemuir, Partick, Falkirk, Killie, Hibs, Motherwell, Dundee Utd, Hearts, Celtic and the Huns all beat us last season (some more than once). We are part of the generation who grew up with Gothenburg, Fergie, cup successes and trouncing the Huns and Celtic on their own patch. They all respected us. Now we were being beaten by the low-lifes of Scottish and European football. We were a joke. Beating us became not so much a battle as a formality. All you had to do was display a reasonable degree of skill mixed with charge of the light brigade type stuff and you could help yourself to the three points.

Why oh why had we reached this lowly level? We could expect our share of defeats in a season, every team could, but not game after game. We were so depressed that demos - treasured memories from the Porterfield and Smith eras - became a complete waste of time. What good would they do? We couldn't demonstrate against Willie could we, after all he had done for our club? Calling for any of the board to get the heave had not borne any positive results in the past.

The despair surrounding all things related to Pittodrie meant that many fans either stopped going or were less vocal than normal at games because they didn't expect us to win. Fewer fans and/or less vocal support means that the team finds it harder to battle out of the position they are in, which makes them more vulnerable, so they get beaten and the doom and gloom enters ever darker shades, and we have our own little vicious circle of blackness.

At least with fear there's an edge and excitement to proceedings as we found out towards the end of the season, but if there's one feeling I never want to experience again - at least over a whole season - it's the one of utter despair that things cannot and will not improve.

Mourning and Guilt

Above all others, a sense of mourning was what affected me the most during the time of Willie Miller's sacking as manager of the club.

This guy, probably the most revered and adored individual in the North East, wasn't producing results. The respect that we all had for him as a man was slowly ebbing away. He couldn't handle the young players; he wouldn't learn from mistakes; he persisted with a crazy defensive system when the world and his wife knew it was a big mistake; there was defeat after defeat; no Jess or Shearer against Skonto Riga. The case for the prosecution was endless.

Most of us knew that he had to go - it was only a matter of when.

The problem was that we were all so desperate for him to succeed that we forgave him his shortcomings until it was too late and we were in relegation trouble.

29

I'll never forget the day he went. The tortured look on his face in the early evening news bulletins told its own story. He looked like he'd just lost a close relative - maybe in a way he had. His eyes were swollen with emotion and his voice barely hid the anger and the pain he was enduring.

I also felt guilty. Guilty for what the club had done to him; guilty for the fans putting him there in the first place; guilty for the players not trying for him; guilty for me wanting him to get the sack three months earlier. I never openly called for the lynch mob, but inside my head I was hoping that he would go gracefully and not suffer the disgrace of the likes of Ian Donald handing him his P45.

You can have all the Ian Donalds and Stewart Milnes and Chris Andersons and Alex Fergusons of this world, but the club will never, never, never, ever have a more loyal and devoted servant than Willie Miller.

Willie's memory as a player will never be tarnished, but sadly the words "sacked as manager" will never be far from his name in the history books.

Togetherness

Union, fellowship, association, accord. The electronic thesaurus threw all these up in my quest to find a suitable emotion to describe the camaraderie we all shared in those final few weeks of season 94/95. In the end I failed and settled for "togetherness" which by my reckoning isn't strictly an emotion, but it's the closest I could come up with.

Talk about bonding. It was like one minute we were against the club, against the board, against the players, against the manager, against each other, and then before you know it we're all in bed shagging the arse off one another.

What happened? Did someone somewhere out there flick a switch or something? It's not as if what we had was tangible, you could feel it but it wasn't something that we all set about acquiring. I guess psychologists would have a name for it. Alexander Dumas coined the phrase "all for one and one for all" and that probably summarises the kindred spirit we developed back then.

We were all in the shit together and each of us knew the price of failure. There have been countless occasions in the past - certainly as long as I have followed the Dons - when one manager or another has come out with the phrase "we must all pull together" after we've had a bad run of results. Usually we ignore this plea and things manage to work out in the end.

Funny thing was, that this time no-one really asked us all to unite - it just happened. Attendances at home games increased and Pittodrie (shock horror) became a noisy place on a Saturday afternoon - at times the decibels grew to such a level with chants of "It's a goal, Duncan Shearer" that one would have expected a petition from the locals. We also managed to eagerly devour our away game ticket allocation, usually doing an Oliver Twist impersonation and going back for more.

On a personal level, I felt that I needed to attend every game in the run-in. Even if it meant the hassle of a midweek jaunt to Fir Park (for another defeat) my heart told me to be there. I would say to myself that if anything was going to happen - for better or worse - I wanted to be there when the time came. There is something quite dark and sinister in that approach if I think about it long enough, so I won't.

Between the months of March and May 1995, mutual respect and trust were conceived within the womb of AFC. The newborn burst forth from the front gates, bawling, screaming and kicking, with two fingers held up at the rest of the world.

Do me a favour. Let's bring up this new creation properly, starting in August 1995.

Relief

Here's a question for you - especially in light of my last emotional outburst on 'togetherness'. What happens when 20,000 Dons fans pull together? Answer: Relief. Ahh yes - 'pulling' and 'relief' - go together like 'Winnie' and 'shite' don't they?

When our second goal went in at East End Park, the weeks of torture were at an end. In some ways for me it was a bit of an anticlimax (could lead you into more double-entendres here but I won't). The nail-biting stuff we had experienced virtually every Saturday for the previous six weeks should have ended, like it would in Roy of the Rovers, with us saving our Premier skins with a last-minute penalty. It's probably just as well that it didn't turn out that way for the St. John's Ambulance crews would surely have had a busy night with hundreds of sheep collapsing with heart attacks.

When Wee Joe's goal went in, it was truly like an enormous weight being lifted from your shoulders. There was no need to worry any more about the fate of this club we all love so dearly. The club that we've all shed tears of joy and disappointment over were finally safe to fight another day in the Premier League.

So, there we were, the final whistle blew and the sun still managed to peer over the stand roof. Below, it cast its fading light on those fans whose relief manifested itself in the form of a pitch invasion. I make no apologies for saying that I was one of those on the pitch. It just seemed the natural thing to do, although I can't really explain why.

The relief for me at any rate, lasted minutes rather than hours. For heading back to the car (on a wayward journey through the streets of Dunfermline with Sparky and my mate Mike navigating???) my thoughts were already turning to next season and what that held in store for us. Since my relief was short-lived, I'll bring this emotion to its end now.

From a Distance

The first season in around 25 years that I've failed to see a single league game, and look what happens. I can hardly yet believe it. When I left for the other side of the globe over two years ago, the team were struggling but even so, I could never have foreseen the slump that came this season.

Two years is a long time in football, to misquote that well-worn phrase. It's easy to lose touch with the players, the new-

comers, those in form and blossoming, and those who have seen
better days. So when the time came to pick a side for Sparky's
Fantasy League, I found myself wondering just who all the
strange names to choose from were. The final selection was based
on a core of players I knew and felt comfortable with, in that I
knew who they were and knew their limitations, so the Pharkin
Nobends XI were:

Dodds (A)
Gough (R)
Hateley (R)
Laudrup (R)
Leighton (Hi)
McCall (R)
McCart (M)
McCoist (R)
McKimmie (A)
McKinnon (A)
Woodthorpe (A)

I'll not try to defend the selection of Gough, Hateley or McCoist.
Suffice to say real money was at stake, and they *did* seem to
have a track record. As a completely unrelated aside, but one
that needs to be told, the When Saturday Comes magazine 1992/
93 offered a couple of specific reasons for readers voting Mark
Hatedly the 'player they'd sooner not meet', most notably because of his 'bad breath' and because 'his jackets cause offence'.
Surprisingly, though, no mention of his lank greasy hair. Bloo
Toon's 'Stench' nickname remains an appropriate favourite of mine.

But why, oh why, did I pick McKimmie? I can't honestly recall,
but the excuse I will offer is that I'd selected my first ten and he
was the only player remaining in the price bracket of the money I
had left to spend.

The omens were good, I thought, when August approached.
World Cup 94 had been pretty entertaining despite the bowf final and had whetted the appetite for the new season, a fresh
start and some interesting new acquisitions.

Unfortunately nobody at Pittodrie was paying any attention
to this fanciful mood of mine.

The season got off to a feeble sort of start, and the message I was getting from home base was one of disappointment, coupled with the usual early-season blind optimism that it was just another typical start-of-season stutter. To a man who is not happy unless he's spouting gloom and doom, there was enough for me to pick up on the little signs of worry and concern and flout my first "Willie must go" mutterings - it didn't take much really. Despite this, the lads were still upbeat enough to tell me to "get real", though I'm sure that the perpetual element of reflex defence in the face of the perennial Hun propaganda from the West Coast media and the resident in-house Impartial Hun played its part in the stand of defiance.

So, their wave of optimism continued and they failed to fully prepare me for the impending shock of actually seeing the Reds in action.

In the two years I'd been living in Jakarta, Indonesia, I'd been back to the UK a couple of times, and managed to get along to Pittodrie on a couple of occasions each time. This year it was a bit more difficult, time was tight and there were so many other things that had to be done and people who had to be seen. However I broke free for a night, dragged along my mate Ian, and headed down to Pittodrie

The saying goes that time makes the heart grow fonder. I don't think so really; a lot of the passion had gone, yet there was still that unexplainable desire and drive to be there, to keep involved, to maintain the interest.

Once thing that time and absence *does* do, though, is rub out the bad memories and enhance the good ones. I entered Pittodrie that chilly night full of fine memories of all the other dramatic European ties that it remains my honour to have witnessed. Just who were this Skonto Riga bunch anyway? A few goals, a chance to see some of the newer faces I hadn't yet seen in action, and a fine pint of ale afterwards to round off a grand night. What could go wrong? The rest, as they say, is history.

I left muttering I had never seen such a poor, disorganised Aberdeen side in all my years at Pittodrie. Not even Bonthrone was guilty of sending out such an inept side. We stumbled home, sneering at the players and angry at being cheated of our gate money.

A rare chance to read the local papers over the next few days, and I was astonished at seeing Jim Dolan have the guts to hit out at the management team and portray a club in trouble. Not astonished because of Dolan's journalistic integrity, but because the cowering P&J had actually allowed the criticism to go to print. Predictably, Jarvie soon tells him to wise up, levers are obviously pulled behind the scenes and Dolan would seem to have been suspended for the rest of the season. The Evening Express allowed the Fat Ex-Postie to happily blubber on, regardless of the unfolding disaster that was clear to all except the managerial incumbents of Pittodrie and to, well, Fat Ex-Posties.

Directors are frequently criticised and laughed at by all and sundry for stating they are in full support of their manager and then sacking him four days later. Well, I too must take issue with the AFC board for publicly stating their support and commitment to Willie but, Christ, our lot bloody-well meant it! Willie and the Board seemed to be the only ones who didn't sense the desperation in the situation, or maybe it was a classic case of self-denial. In any case it couldn't go on, really. But it did.

So with this picture in mind I flew back South for the winter, more bearable temperatures. Well, someone has to pioneer and develop these barren oil patches despite the hardships of living in a developing country and having to look after a household of servants.

There is an incredible thirst for information, and deep frustration at the lack of available in-depth detail and rumour, in being a long-distance supporter. I stopped calling myself a fan immediately after being put in my place by the shiny-headed Early Ball. Upon asking me one day many moons ago if I was heading down to Pittodrie on the Saturday, I confirmed that indeed I was. "I wouldn't mind seeing the Hearts", I mentioned (it happened to be during one of their mini-revivals). Early Ball rounded on me instantly, saying, *"that* was the difference between me and the rest of the other lads." A fan goes to see his own team play, regardless of who the opposition is or the importance of the match. Seemingly I was a *football* supporter first and foremost, who just happened to side with AFC. Fair enough, I suppose.

Unfortunately my access to Scottish footie information was limited to the BBC World Service sports roundup at 5:45 every morning or the occasional well-hidden one liner in The Jakarta Post. This was supplemented by a weekly delivery of Scotland on Sunday, posted faithfully by Old Beach Ender every week and arriving in time for reading over the following weekend. For this I am immensely grateful to him. Another weekly source of information was The British Soccer Weekly, an Australian publication, and subscribed to by a Spurs supporter working alongside me. But there is no substitute for immediacy and quantity of information, and daily updates on injuries, transfer speculation and dressing room bust-ups were denied me.

I can't claim to have been starved of football entirely, mind you. Coverage of the world game is excellent in this football-loving nation. Football coverage in Indonesia consists of an English game live every Saturday night, with Italian, Dutch and English games live on the Sunday night. This is supplemented by an Indonesian league game live every Saturday and Sunday afternoon. Okay, so the quality of the local game may leave a lot to be desired but this season saw an incident that will surely grace the Question of Sport screens sometime in the future.

It is chucking it down in a typical tropical thunderstorm in the middle of the rainy season, when one of the players gets injured. The ref. takes a quick peek and waves the trainer on. He scampers across the muddy pitch until he gets about ten yards from the stricken forward, at which point he ends up on his back sliding along the ground and sticks his flailing boot into the face of the grounded player, strangely enough not unlike the 'accidental' maiming of Theo's cheek by Sally McMoist many moons ago. The floored player had to be stretchered off. Look out for it.

It was hardly reassuring stuff, early to mid season. The usual draws, sprinkled with close defeats and hammerings of Falkirk and Dundee Utd, and a three game run of defeats against Motherwell, Hearts and Celtic. The season was beginning to take shape. Shadows were beginning to be cast over Pittodrie. Yet loyalty to Willie barely wavered.

November came and there was another three game run of defeats, Partick, Rangers and, yes, Killie. This must finally, surely, signal the inclusion of a P45 in Willie's pay packet?

But no. 1995 approached and we entered the New Year with lighter moods yet again, having once more humbled the mighty Hearts with a 3-1 drubbing. The corner was turned, there was a new dawn, a fresh start, a clean sheet, and all that jazz. Well, there was a clean sheet right enough for the first couple of games of 1995, titillating goalless draws against Falkirk and the Arabs. An undefeated run of four games. "Crisis? What crisis?", hooted the Aberdeen management team and the Willie die-hards.

Scotland on Sunday, and the occasional Sunday Mason I got my hands on, were adamant. Every manager interviewed (except the myopic John Lambie who didn't want to discuss AFC) were in agreement. All the players said so too. It couldn't happen to Aberdeen, relegation that is, because Aberdeen are just too good a club to be relegated.

Even now, I can't believe anyone could say that. I'd seen them play Skonto for crying out loud. I *knew* it was bullshit. Besides, everyone in the mire and dog-fight with us had been through it before. They knew what a relegation battle was all about, they knew it was a case of rolling the sleeves up and getting the backsides dirty with desperate tackles. They weren't going to roll over and play dead for a fellow struggler, no matter what their pedigree or supposed standing in the Scottish game. We *all* knew that, but maybe some just preferred, or hoped, or simply wanted to believe it couldn't happen, and needed the reassurance of being told so. I don't know, but I just felt like I wanted to get back to Aberdeen and shake some sense into those airheads.

A narrow win over mighty Stranraer and yet another defeat at the hands of powerful Killie.

Willie continued his King Canute impersonation. Confusion reigned. Should he or shouldn't he? Will he or won't he? Had he or hadn't he?

He wouldn't. So he was shoved.

The club were firmly rooted at the bottom. There was not the slightest glimmer of a turn-around. *There Was No Hope.* He had to go, and should have gone sooner. Surely everyone could see that.

Strange, then, to note the shock, sadness and anger that was expressed by the majority of fans. I can only think it had to be one of those occasions when you just had to be there to experience it. It must have been some sight to see our long-standing God near to tears and answering questions in a quiet near-breaking voice. For me, Willie's sacking was viewed in a totally detached and unemotional manner. Sure, he was the club's best-ever playing servant, and because of his playing career I will continue to forever hold him in awe and respect. But the truth is, if he had remained until the season's end I don't believe anyone genuinely thinks he could have turned the team round the way Aitken did, and he just had to go. Whether Aitken is really the right choice for job in the long term I have my reservations, but will give the man a chance. He deserves that, at least, for his end-of-season achievements.

A lot of the sensible arguments were made about the timing of the dismissal, and here I'll agree with the majority, he really should have gone much sooner in the season. I'd not have been too upset to see him to go after the Skonto game, as I said, or at least after losing the December match to Kilmarnock. It had gone on too long by that point already. It was clear to most onlookers that nothing was improving, or even ever likely to improve.

Opinion was now divided. Old loyalties were being strained. Still, a good 2-0 thumping of the evil filthy Huns proved it was all just a bad dream and unleashed more outpourings of, yes, Aberdeen were just too good a side to go down. Funny how the dogs turned later though.......

The Stenhousemuir game came and went (enough said) and the season effectively ended in terms of opportunities for genuine glory.

Draws against Partick and Hibs. We were all getting desperate. Surely it was past the point of no-return and the changes on the managerial front had come too late and at too crucial a time in the season?

The same people who had been telling us all season that Aberdeen were too good a side to go down were suddenly now telling us that Aberdeen would definitely be relegated because they were just so bad. For God's sake, we always knew that, we just didn't want them to be telling us that *now,* in our darkest hour. If players and managers can be charged with bringing the game into disrepute, why not journalists and commentators? Some of what was, and continues to be written by these hacks is a disgrace.

At least John Lambie was of a consistent mind. He still wasn't interested in talking about AFC.

Saturday nights saw me becoming extremely unsociable. Now I was sitting watching the live English League game with the short-wave radio plugged into the ear-holes, glued to Paddy Feeney of the World Service's Sportsworld programme running through the latest scores.

39

Roddy Forsyth continued to gloat over every Hun win and each Aberdeen defeat on the World Service. Within the guy uttering two words on a match report, you could tell the result. The cheery welcome, the bounce in the voice.... the evil filthy Huns had won and/or Aberdeen had lost. By the end of the season I was writing letters to the World Service's Regional Head of Programming asking for his removal.

Everyone was getting depressed and more and more frantic. Platitudes by well-meaning people saying that, well, maybe a season in the first division would be good for the club, were met with pointed responses from me. Mindless rubbish.

The Pharkins were no source of Fantasy League comfort either. McMoist was injured, Hatedly was injured, Gough was injured, and half my side were out at one time or another. In the top quarter, but not likely to make a Eurodollar spot.

AFC stumbled on through two draws (Partick and Hibs) before the mighty Killie achieved the dreadful distinction of a fourth league win over us during the season. John the token Jakarta Killie supporter didn't rub it in right away, though. He waited until first thing Monday before calling and laughing down the phone.

The start of April also saw a major disaster on the news front. The BBC revamped their programme schedules and a casualty was the 5:45 am sports roundup. My major daily source of news had dried up. By the time the next edition was broadcast I was usually in the car on the way to work.

Thankfully OBE came to the rescue. He informed me of some Internet services that might be useful; Scottish results and an Aberdeen discussion group. This, coupled with costly calls to UK-based telephone results' services, managed to fill most of the gaps.

Roy's Plodders faced a tricky match against his old club during a weekend which saw the Nervuz family being invited up to a bungalow in the Puncak, a mountainous area south of Jakarta and a chance for some cool fresh air, with temperatures a much more pleasant 80F. Thankfully Carol and Ian McKenzie, our delightful hosts, understood the agonies of being a Dons fan with Ian being a bit of a closet Aberdeen man himself. Social politeness went out the window on the Saturday at 9pm (six hours ahead of BST) as the well-worn radio was whipped out of the bag, much to my wife's annoyance at my lack of good manners, and the two of us huddled round the wee box, ears trying to sift out Paddy Feeney from the crackled reception.

The omens weren't good. Thunder and lightning filled the air, the electricity went off and the candlelight ambience went well with the cans of Tiger beer. Straight out of a Hammer horror movie. But I needn't have worried. The lads did the bizz for Roy and once again hopes were raised. Things had changed again and now we would win our remaining games, surely.

The 2-1 defeat at the hands of Motherwell set us straight yet again and saw old Paddy Feeney passing a heartfelt comment. "This is all rather amazing, we have an annual sweep in the office and everyone to a man, and woman, had Aberdeen as first or second", he said. Tell me about it, Paddy.

Luckily the BBC seemed to have cottoned on to Roddy Forsyth and little was heard from the odious reporter during the run-in to the season's end.

The Hearts game arrived. Make or break and, through the Aberdeen Internet group, I could sense a spirit of brotherhood amongst the Aberdeen fans. No-one can forget how the game went, and it's impossible to describe how my stomach twisted each time Paddy Feeney handed over to Tynecastle for the latest update. The joy of the opening goal, the expectation of a bigger lead at the announcement of a second goal at Tynecastle, and the anxious seconds as we endured a two-minute replay of the commentary buildup as play swung from end to end before realising it was a bloody equaliser. Anxious nail-biting and an explosion of utter relief as our second went in late in the game.

The Fantasy League was lost to me, but the Fantasy Cup, sponsored by The Red Final, was well underway; Pharkin had successfully negotiated the opening rounds and were into the quarterfinals. Losing finalists last year, we'd a cup tradition to live up to. There was a lot at stake. Well, fifty quid actually.

So now it was all down to the Dundee Utd game. Sad really, as I'd always had a wee bit of a soft spot for the Arabs. There were many thoroughly enjoyable European evenings that Ian and I had spent at Tannadice during the 'New Firm' glory days, including the unforgettable thrashing of Borussia Munchengladbach. (Who's the most hated fan in Munich? The guy who starts the chant 'Give us a B-ee-ee'. The old ones are the best, eh?). But sentiment played no part in the buildup, and the Tangerine Dream just had to become a nightmare (*who writes this stuff?-Ed*).

I realised I was in tricky waters on Friday night. The wife reminded me that we were going to a ceilidh the next evening. There is a very healthy St. Andrews Society in Jakarta with a whole host of events to make sure you don't forget about home. And so it was I found myself at a club by the banks of a river in temperatures in the 90's, surrounded by traditionalists wearing kilts and dancing eightsome reels and the like. The discussion at our table was nearly all about football, as it should be. As the thirsts were more than quenched, and time passed, my thoughts were all at Pittodrie. The radio had been left behind, thinking that some of the other die-hards who I knew were attending would be bringing theirs. As bad luck would have it, everyone thought the same, and we were stranded with no connection to Paddy Feeney.

Full-time must have been blown and I was desperate to know. A Raith fan at our table was also desperate to know how Raith had got on. Eventually, without too much persuasion really, I got him to go to his car, get his portable phone and call his family in Scotland.

Unbelievably he got through first time (the Indonesian phone system isn't the best in the world) and even more unbelievably I had to endure Alan first asking about the Raith score and having a five-minute discussion on the game before he almost hung up without asking the only score that really mattered, attention being diverted from the mundane to more important matters as I bounced frantically beside him and threatened to empty his pint glass.

2-0 was the reply. It turned out to be the wrong result, I later discovered, but thankfully the points were still ours. I was a mighty happy man for the rest of the night, and just as happy again on Monday at finding Pharkin had made it through to The Red Final Fantasy Cup Final.

In many ways, the Falkirk game was a bit of an anticlimax for the long-distance supporter. It was difficult to get caught up in the excitement when you're not surrounded by it all each and every day. The game had its moments for those of us glued to our trannies. Knowing that Big Alex's side only needed to take a point off Hearts to ensure we avoided the play-offs, I was quite confident that our longtime hero would give us a helping hand.

With only minutes to go, the play-offs were looming despite reports of Motherwell pressure at Tynecastle. And then a few seconds of utter torture. "And there's news of a penalty at Tynecastle", announces Paddy. "Surely, oh surely, Murrawell must score", I thought. It never crossed my mind for a second that the penalty could be for Hearts. Of course the dirty pseudo-Huns put it away and the wee dreams faded.

The Dons' dramatic end of season recovery played a large part in the Pharkins' cup run, and another fine set of results that weekend saw them lift their first ever trophy. The Red Final Trophy is nestling proudly in the deepest drawer of my office. The £50 cheque was most welcome as well. Ya beauty, McKimmie had come good!

Fortunes had turned. If only the lads could finish the play-off in the first leg at Pittodrie......

Finish it they duly did, and the second leg was a formality. The relief was long overdue.

So Aitken managed to achieve the miracle that most of us at one point or another thought unlikely and kept AFC's proud record intact. I'm convinced that the man has a back garden full of four-leaf clovers. At the time of writing there is a great deal of uncertainty over who will and won't be staying on at the club for the new season. Whatever happens, Roy needs to get some new blood in.

If the proposed Share Offer comes off, and gets the support from the fans it deserves, then the money may well be there for him to spend. The mood is right for the start of a new era.

The wind of change that is blowing down Merkland Road could yet strengthen to gale force.

The Press

Throughout a season of grinding frustration and mind-bog glingly poor quality football (from everybody, not just us), capped by a wonderful and crucially successful burst of passionate determination from everybody associated with the Dons: players, fans, backroom staff, board and local community, there was one abiding certainty - the press and media were revelling in the club's discomfiture, with the Glasgow press, as ever, being by far the worst offenders.

It all began in a positive and optimistic light. Kevin McCarra of 'Scotland on Sunday' produced an article at the outset of the season, including an interview with Willie Miller, which waxed lyrical about the restructuring of the team, with a clearout of older players whose legs were gone or going and their replacement with new, younger faces. Everything looked set for the Dons to make a competitive assault on the early season and indeed stay the pace to be the now traditional main, or only, serious rivals to the much-loathed Huns. I have to confess to penning an article for Scottish football's venerable fanzine, 'The Absolute Game', in which I speculated that the Dons were really going to get into gear after the dismal, draw-stuffed, preceding season and even went as far as to say I'd be popping into the bookies for a flutter on our chances of hauling in some silverware. We were all set to settle into an exciting season full of northeastern promise.

Then the new season started for real and the roof caved in, in immediate and dramatically painful fashion, setting fans and club reeling in a way that none of us had experienced before.

Jim Dolan of the 'Press & Journal' was quickly off his mark in sounding out a warning of what was to come. Before the return match against Skonto Riga, he produced a piece headlined 'Alarm Bells Should Be Ringing at Pittodrie' in which he warned that Aberdeen's start to the season should be giving the management at Pittodrie far more than mere food for thought. In a refreshingly honest and realistic piece of writing, something readers were not accustomed to seeing in the local papers, Dolan set out in plain English the glaring problems which Aberdeen were creating for themselves. He pointed out the folly of the new defensive 3-5-2/5-3-2 (no one was ever sure which) formation and questioned the attitude of players who had already struggled to beat Stranraer and stuttered to a scary two-all draw with Falkirk, a team that should normally be expected to suffer heavily at the hands of the Dons.

The press speculation about Willie Miller's tenure as manager began in earnest after the Riga humiliation, and we were subjected to, or entertained by an unceasing barrage right up to Miller's sacking in February. As things got worse in the League, the press clamour of attention became frenzied as, like a school of underfed, petulant Piranha fish, the hacks from Glasgow delved into every conceivable cranny to get an angle on Aberdeen's tormented season. The amazing thing about it was that for the first time in years, possibly ever, Aberdeen were dominating the back pages to the extent that they were actually keeping Rangers and Celtic away from their traditional, high-profile press exposure.

The reportage wasn't all bad, and amazingly there were some excellent interviews with former players published, giving their personal insights into what was the matter at Pittodrie. The bottom line though, was that the Glasgow-published newspapers simply could not hide their delight that the Dons, who had once had the temerity to come to the forefront of Scottish and European football at the expense of the vastly overrated 'Old Firm', were now in trouble and indeed facing the threat of relegation. Aberdeen's fans, showing an incredible personal loyalty to Willie Miller, were quick to recognise the hostility from Glasgow's west end bull pits, which wasn't really anything new, and by November they launched the defiant and oft repeated "Are you watching Glasgow press?" song which was reprised with increasing frequency as the season neared its end and the Dons finally found their feet.

The ongoing catalogue of animosity between the Glasgow Press and Aberdeen was already legendary and was compounded now by the relentless attempts of the hacks to make this past season far worse than it already was. We were subjected to a diarrhoea of poisonous kite flying, taking, in the main, the form of utterly unfounded transfer stories - easily spotted in print by their complete lack of any attributed "quotations" whatsoever - the 'Daily Ranger' being a leading exponent of this tactic. The new "Scottish" Mail even unearthed the old chestnut of the 'Durrant/Simpson' story for its debut edition and repeated the calumny later in the season.

What the sleazy denizens of the dilapidated press boxes of Scotland really hoped or expected to achieve, other than causing mild irritation all round, is hard to imagine. If they thought that their childish tactics were going to help us on our way to a lower league, they were patently mistaken. For certain, there was going to be no significant impact on the players who were named in these exercises in rumour mongering; it is hard to imagine that a story claiming that one player or another wanting to move on would affect his team-mates in any way, beyond giving them some material for winding each other up, especially since the people best placed to know the truth of what was really going on were the players themselves. The intention may have been simply to keep the Hun, Tim and other minority clubs' readerships happy, but the maliciousness will never be forgotten by Aberdeen supporters nor the club and there are many so called 'football writers' who should never be welcomed across the threshold of Pittodrie Stadium again.

Aberdeen Journals' newspapers were a bit flummoxed by this season, and the 'Evening Express' in particular, even once it had admitted there was a problem, floundered around trying to lay blame everywhere but the right place for a long time. The 'Press & Journal' was generally more up to the task of saying what had to be said but unfortunately they spoilt it all with their 'We're Backing the Dons' campaign which mainly took the form of local businessmen telling us how important it was to local commerce that AFC should perform well and preferably successfully. The effect of a successful football team on business or productivity may well be a factor of life, but it really wasn't what fans or players wanted or needed to be reading on the back page of the paper day in and day out. Fortunately that campaign fizzled out after a while and only the logo continued to appear up till the end of the season.

Over at the TV stations, the pattern was a little different, in that whilst STV's leading Hun sycophant, simpering Jim White, could barely keep the oily smirk of delight from his rapidly ageing features, at the BBC there was a modest degree of restraint and even, on occasion, a slight hint that Dougie Donnely was taking a nearly neutral stance. The fact that neither station was bothering to cover the Dons' matches very much was a contributing factor and of course STV's famous reluctance to attend anything other than Rangers' games (even mentioned in the 'Daily Ranger') meant that they were only able to bring the Dons to their screens on a limited number of occasions. However, the STV pundits didn't actually do a jig around the studio when the subject of AFC's plight came up, but they must have been sorely tempted. Gerry McNee did manage to spray unhelpful twaddle around the nation, but in his case, probably no one noticed the difference from his usual outpourings. Astonishingly, smirking Derek Johnstone managed to appear almost sympathetic on 'Sportscene' and even spouted the odd constructive remark that, whilst hardly putting him in our camp, at least indicated that he wasn't going to put the boot in on Saturday evenings.

Never having listened to Radio Clyde's sports programme, I can't really say too much about their behaviour, although with Archie McPherson and chortling Chic Young participating it's not too hard to imagine what sort of bull would have been on offer if they ever managed to tear themselves away from the Hun reserve matches at Ibrox. The same can't be said about Clyde's cousin Northsound. Already committed to a two year sponsorship deal with the Dons, the station and more particularly many of its broadcasters, demonstrated a healthy degree of local patriotism with DJs as well as local sports programmes getting behind the Dons, often with tremendous humour, enthusiasm and sound constructive comment, thus providing some respite for beleaguered Rudolphs. Nice one lads.

Perhaps the greatest airing of the Dons' troubles was given by BBC Radio Scotland's 'Sportsound' programme, with the debates amongst their regular pundits totalling many hours. It was on this programme that the idea of reorganising the League to ensure the Dons' 'safety' was first put forward - an idea which didn't meet with any great enthusiasm from many quarters including Dons' fans, but which Dundee United might now be wishing had been followed through more vigorously. 'Sportsound' actually went as far as to invite an Aberdeen fan, Paul Thomson no less, onto the programme to join the debate and give the supporters' point of view. In a classic piece of broadcasting, Paul not only managed to put the fans' case but also to put the gloomily unhelpful Jim Traynor of 'The Herald' in his place on a few matters. At least on this show, we had guys whom we knew were genuine sympathisers and although Richard Gordon maintained a relatively restrained, neutral stance in his role of anchorman, he still managed to do his bit for our cause and of course Joe Harper didn't hold back with his views.

Latterly, Willie Miller took a job with 'Sportsound' and inevitably was brought into the discussions. On the whole, whilst never admitting there had been anything wrong with his approach to management, he maintained a dignified, diplomatic stance and wasn't drawn too much by all attempts to get him to stir it. Until, that is, the day of the Falkirk game when, after hearing Ian

Donald expressing relief that the Dons had made it to the play-offs and claiming that the turnaround of recent weeks justified Willie's sacking, Miller finally and unhelpfully gave vent to his feelings about the Aberdeen board.

Having travelled this far in the recovery process, having at long last strung some wins together, having demonstrated a new found will to win and seen the unity amongst fans, players and board, you might have thought that at this stage the press would have started taking a look at what had happened to pull us around and offered some little credit for it - but no. What we got was sketchy bad publicity for Aberdeen fans over their behaviour at Falkirk, followed by a barrage of publicity for Dunfermline people, mostly their manager Bert Paton, whining about having to face us in the play-offs. We even got the Simpson/Durrant business aired yet again. Clearly the enemy had not sated themselves on their season-long joyride of AFC suffering and hoped somehow that we would still collapse at the last minute to a Dunfermline team that was on a fifteen game unbeaten run.

Of course, all that Dunfermline's whinging achieved from our point of view was to demonstrate that, in their minds at least, they were already beaten and although they did play with a lot of vigour at Pittodrie and early on at East End Park, there was only ever going to be one winner. Mind you, even after that first play-off game, the press were more intent on whining about a penalty that they deemed Dunfermline deserved rather that any achievement of the Dons. Strangely there was no mention of the penalties that **we** might have had, but then we're used to that with these scum bags - aren't we?

In the end, the last game was so close to the Cup Final that the majority of the media had a solid excuse to ignore the fact that the Dons had managed to save themselves and apart from a few bitchy remarks about fans celebrating on that last night of our season and hooligans invading the pitch, they dropped the story of the season like an overheated thing that you couldn't hold onto even if you wanted to. They couldn't understand that people stayed long after the end of that game in Dunfermline singing and chanting not in celebration but in relief at finally evading the spectre of relegation for the first time in Aberdeen FC's history, a relief that we wanted to share with the players. Instead, the hacks tried to turn our behaviour on that night into

49

something shameful and none of us were surprised, none of us were hurt, none of us expected anything else.

Over the season I had some personal brushes with the media, which I will now share with you but which you can easily dodge by skipping to the last paragraph. First off the blocks was Grampian TV's Donald John MacDonald who came to record a short interview on the day Willie Miller was sacked. This was before the sacking and I went on record as saying that Willie should go. Events took over and I didn't make my screen debut. Shortly after that Ian Campbell of the 'Daily Ranger' (his own words as well as ours) 'phoned to get a reaction to the sacking. I know, I know, I should have told anybody involved with that rag to sod off, but Campbell is a fairly decent bloke and known as a Dundee United supporter so I relented and told him about having to rewrite 'The Red Final' editorial several times in the space of twenty four hours because of rapidly changing events. His report touched on the conversation, but he chose to be a bit sarcastic, claiming (wrongly) that we'd be out of date by the time that edition hit the streets.

Radio took over after that and BBC Radio Four sent a news reporter to ask me what had gone wrong. The interview was hacked down to a couple of minutes and broadcast one Saturday morning at a speed that made me sound like I was on helium; that didn't matter though, the point is that I got a fair hearing from that particular quarter. Next up, courtesy of Mad Mac of 'The Absolute Game', I was invited to take part in Ruth Wishart's 'Speaking Out' programme on Radio Scotland. This involved sitting in splendid isolation in the BBC's Aberdeen studios whilst Partick-supporting (allegedly) Ruth and the other guests, George Fulston of Falkirk and Alan McGraw of Morton, sat round a table in Glasgow. Boy is it hard to get a word in. The discussion was supposed to be about the state of Scottish football and the need or otherwise for change, but the Dons' problems came up several times and I had a bit of a falling-out with Ms. Wishart when she spoke as though we were already relegated. I didn't like that and politely corrected her. We also fell out when she put a hypothetical question to me about whether I'd go and watch them if there was a freeze on promotion and relegation - she didn't seem to think that trying to win the championship was in itself terribly relevant and thereby managed to demonstrate that she knew nothing whatever about supporting a team. On the whole though, I felt that when

the Dons were mentioned I managed to go to bat for them reason-
ably well and certainly didn't let them down - don't think I'll be
asked back though.

The last segment of this wee flurry of media whoredom was a
chat with Radio Five, in company with Sparky, outside Pittodrie
on the eve of the Dundee United game. Like their Radio Four
cousin, 'Five Live' gave us a fair hearing and were a good example
of the way sport should be reported. Incidentally, I'm sure that it
was only coincidence that Willie Miller (whose contribution to
the programme was taped) turned up in the car park next to us
whilst we were on air. I'm sure he was only there to use the golf
driving range and not keep an eye on us. Anyway, more power to
BBC Radio and Northsound, because they were the only parts of
the media which behaved decently throughout the season so far
as the Dons and their supporters were concerned.

There has been a long running enmity between the supporters of Aberdeen Football Club and the 'West Coast Mafia' (the
existence of which, unsurprisingly, they vehemently deny) and
the Dons' fanzines have railed against the hacks long and loud.
Now the dust of our longest season is settling and the Dons are
still in the Premier League, but the war of words goes on. If ever
you need an extra excuse, or reminding of why you should stand
firmly behind the Dons, just borrow somebody else's copy of one of
the rags produced amongst Glasgow's sleazy back street slums,
turn to the back pages and scan the biased trash they are serving
up in place of balanced football coverage. I rest my case.

No Willie

The trauma endured on certain occasions disturbs personal stability to such an extent that the date becomes as much a part of your being as your internal or other vital organs. It is for this reason, combined with the desire to continue with life, that most of us remember things like our wedding anniversary. The bigger the personal trauma, the more significance the date assumes. The 18th of September 1970, for instance, had such an affect on my (only just) adolescent soul that for years I would prolong the pain by inserting a small In Memorium advert in the P & J. All because James Marshall Hendrix passed away that day and the world has since been deprived of his brilliance. While I recognise that this date will mean nothing to those who feel that the only music worth listening to is by Fuck That, there is little doubt that some sodden-gusseted nymphette will, by the time she becomes a hingin'-gowled thirty-something, remember with stunning clarity the date that one of her erstwhile heroes got married or died from prolonged and excessive production of mediocrity. She may even insert an advert in The Peoples' Friend to commemorate the event.

But dates mean even more to footie fans. Blue-clad neanderthals regularly proclaim the importance of the 12th of July and you can rest assured that someone claiming Irish descent will have the date of the Bunnet McGoo/Parkhead revolution as firmly implanted in his or her tiny skull as the words to "The Soldier's Song" or whatever it's called.

Kilmarnock supporters almost certainly know the exact date in 1965 when they last clinched the league and even fans of lesser known clubs such as Dynamo New Byth Academicals will no doubt be proud to tell you the date of their magnificent retention of the Mains of Flechie Beast Memorial Trophy, or the injury time defeat in the Rag, Scrap And Metal Merchants' Cup.

Aberdeen fans? The 3rd of May 1980 when a 5-0 victory at Easter Road brought us the first league title since the Pope was an altar boy and sent us dancing around the HIV capital.

The 16th March 1983, when Bayern Munich were well and truly stuffed in a match which had the best atmosphere I've ever witnessed at Pittodrie.

The 11th of May 1983 when I discovered heaven was called the Ullevi Stadium.

More recently, there was the 6th May 1995, a game against Dundee Utd when defeat for either side meant relegation. Our 2-1 victory led to scenes of joy unseen for many a year, even though it was quite possible that AFC could still be relegated if they failed in their remaining games. I for one will never forget the atmosphere in The Blue Lamp, when among other wheezes, one worthy stood on the bar and pretended to ride a motor bike, while the rest of the crowd whistled or hummed the theme tune to The Great Escape. These are only examples and I'm sure everyone has their own favourites.

On the other side of the coin is the 11th May 1991 when a bit of Hateley hooliganism and a typical combination of inept tactics and irresolute team selection robbed us of a title that in all truth we weren't really good enough to claim.

This season has claimed another dark day in the shape of the 6th of February 1995. This was the day Aberdeen sacked Willie Miller.

I believe this will become the Dons equivalent of the Kennedy question (22/11/63, or so I'm told). "Where were you and what were you doing when you heard the fateful news?" Fans everywhere will remember in minute detail, such was the gravity of the event. Me ? I was sitting in the car waiting for No. 1 daughter to return from an appointment when my radio seemed to announce the news in the same slow motion that accompanies historic catastrophe or vital headed goals. I knew something was brewing when I drove past Pittodrie at lunchtime and observed the number of sports writers hanging around outside. (What is the correct descriptive term for a collection of sports reporters? A plagiary? A column? A chapter? An illegitimacy? An illiteracy? In Scotland it must be an Ibrox, which just about sums up the combination of intellectual ability, moral deficiency, and geographical orientation required to be successful in that dubious profession, with few but notable exceptions.) In fact, the numbers hanging around suggested that this was a veritable Govan of hacks and they had the same demeanour as pigs setting out on a truffle hunt, hounds in pursuit of a fox or a hun supporter attempting to understand adult conversation. They knew something valuable was there but they couldn't quite get to it.

I drove past the stadium on several occasions that tension-laden afternoon, trying to communicate something telepathically to the Board that ultimately holds the increasingly desperate reins of my hopes and dreams. Just what it was I wanted to communicate, I'm not entirely sure. I was determined, however, to exert just a little influence, even if it was just to scream something obscene or simply convey a shake of the head in disbelief at an increasingly grotesque pattern of events, in what had become a surreal season of Dada-esque proportions.

So when the news broke, I sat back and breathed a sigh of relief, which contained enough acerbity to fill the sky, a mountain of wrath and an ocean of anguish. (Clichéd? Pretentious? Fa' me?) This maelstrom of emotions remained with me for some considerable time, causing my popularity rating with the rest of the domestic clan to plummet from an already low point. (What do they know about the important things in life?)

Radio Scotland happened to be covering a cup tie involving, (naturally), other teams that evening but some wanted to concentrate on the importance of the decision, no doubt aided by the Reds' cavalry, in the shape of Richard Gordon, who happens to be the exception that proves the rule about west-coast media bias. He had no doubt of the momentous nature of events but unfortunately Bob Crampsey, Alec Cameron et al, gave the impression they were speaking about the unfortunate demise of a distant relative's pet hamster. I felt so upset at their incapacity to grasp what Willie Miller's departure might mean to a Reds' fan that I wrote to Gordon Smith the following day in a naive attempt to rectify the situation.

To my surprise, he actually replied some time later and included an article he had written for the 'Scottish Sunday Express', which made several points concurring with my own point of view. Unfortunately, he ruined some good work by trying to claim that a West Coast Mafia did not exist, which just goes to show how you can be too close to something to recognise its existence, never mind appreciate the scale of its depravity. Despite this, what he had to say about Willie's departure made a lot of sense. This may lead to the, hitherto unthinkable, conclusion that a headline describing my feelings might read "Dons Fan Agrees With Ex-Hun Who Writes For Right Wing Broadsheet Shock".

Somewhat surprisingly, you might think, given the tone of what I've already written. I should make it clear that, in my view, Miller had long been a liability as manager and I expressed that view in TRF in November 1994. I had serious doubts about his ability to successfully manage the club for considerably longer than that. So why did I react with such angst, despair and frustration when the Board delivered its P45-shaped Exocet? Having argued so vehemently for his departure isn't it just a tad hypocritical to moan when it happens? It might be, but this is a complicated picture, coloured by large amounts of emotion for all AFC fans, which goes some way to explaining the reaction of many since the event.

For me, an analogy might be the case of someone who is very

55

close to you who has a terminal illness. It's obvious to everyone that he's not going to get better and you wish with all your heart that the suffering will quickly be over. When it does happen you're consumed by guilt at having such cruel thoughts and it's only with the benefit of hindsight that you realise that striving beyond the call of duty to keep someone alive is not to the benefit of the patient, even if he has sworn to fight the illness to the very end. All it does is stop the relatives grieving for their own loss at an earlier stage. Those who hoped that Miller would never be sacked are the same people who would keep someone alive in the hope that a wonder drug will appear at the last moment, thus ruling out their need to grieve. Unfortunately, life, like football management, ain't like that. It's here that the analogy ends, the victim's still with us, at least in spirit and he obviously retains a deep love for AFC, if not for the people who run it. It's this that makes the whole situation difficult to take.

That Willie Miller is the greatest player ever to play for Aberdeen is not a controversial statement. We should remember that no player of similar stature has ever dedicated an entire career to what has long been considered by all but the Reds' cognoscenti and the occasional rational journo, as a club that will only occasionally challenge for honours. For twenty-odd years this guy was the best penalty box defender around. What's often forgotten is the number of times when his frustrations at the inabilities or lack of imagination of those playing in front of him drove him to stride up the park with the ball, almost daring the opposition to make a tackle. Usually, this ended in a dead ball situation deep in the opposing half, when a hapless defender was forced to bring him down or thump the ball behind for a corner. Miller would then present the familiar granite-faced scowl to his team mates, as if to say, "Christ, have I got to do **all** the work?" As usual, leading by example.

On a couple of occasions, his forays up field led to more spectacular results. One of the best goals I've ever seen was scored by Miller. Against Hibs, on 29th February 1978, in a match played in the thickest fog since Basil Rathbone strutted his stuff as a seven per cent solution-free Sherlock, Miller bounded upfield before completing a series of one-twos on the edge of the box, riding a desperate tackle and slamming the ball into the onion bag. Stunning stuff, Archie, and wasn't it just his luck that the nation was deprived of this bit of brilliance because the TV cameras couldn't penetrate the fog? In another game at Pittodrie, on 27th April 1985, he scored a goal against Celtic which led to us clinching the league, and he celebrated just as much as we did. There was much, much more than this and we should never forget it. That he stayed with AFC despite offers from all over the place is probably even more important.

Turning down a move to the huns only heightened his stature in the eyes of those who have enough sense to realise that the promised land is not located in Govan. There are several ex-Aberdeen players who could have gone on to similar status with AFC but decided to abscond elsewhere, notably, Martin Buchan and Gordon Strachan. They chose to move elsewhere and both succeeded in building very successful careers. Had Willie Miller chosen to bugger off somewhere similar in search of more shekels and fame, and nobody would have been too surprised if he had, he too would now be held in the same awe as these two are in England. We should remember that, and be eternally grateful that he decided to stick with us.

What happened, then, when he finished his playing career, and where did it all go wrong? It was entirely right that such loyalty should be rewarded with a permanent place on the staff and initially, it seemed that the youth and reserve players were getting the benefit of Miller's expertise and enthusiasm. Attendances at reserve games were rewarded by a fit young team playing the sort of skilful but wholesome football which all the quality sides in Scotland have produced in recent years. This was accompanied by enthusiasm, encouragement and obvious commitment from the dugout, qualities notably absent from Miller's equivalents during first team games. It is, perhaps, at this point that a combination of circumstances became apparent that was ultimately to lead to the demise of one of AFC's greatest and most respected employees.

Arguably, more than enough has been written regarding the Reds' performances under Alex Smith, but given that the pundits, regarded by the intellectually challenged as unequalled in their knowledge of Scottish football, continually give "dewy-eyed" (thank you, Sparky) accounts of the greatness achieved under his management, perhaps a few last words are in order, in an attempt to wither the reason for the horizontal sporran (thank you, Count) which seems to appear whenever the (nowhere near Glasgow) Herald's Jim Traynor and his contemptible peers mention Alex Smith's name.

In season 89/90, AFC win the Skol Cup 2-1 against the huns in extra time and the Scottish Cup 9-8, against Celtic, in a penalty shoot-out. They were beaten in the first round of the UEFA Cup by Rapid Vienna. Their league form was patchy, with some excellent football at times and some of the direst pish imaginable at others. The end of the season saw us as runners up to a poor huns team in the championship by a margin of seven points. This looks on paper to be quite impressive but anybody watching them knew that the play didn't have the majesty that the quality of player on the books should have produced. It seemed to most that any good performances happened despite, not because of, managerial intervention.

The following season, Aberdeen continued their lacklustre league form with a series of performances which lacked commitment but which were defended by Smith on the basis of defensive visiting teams and injuries, a tale we were to hear much more of in seasons to come. That Aberdeen played some of the most defensive football seen by the support for many years, particularly in away games, seemed to pass Smith by. Unfortunately, it was all too clear to those who watched them regularly that there was a lack of imagination in their play that would have been unthinkable only a few short years before.

The Reds were beaten 1-0 in the Skol Cup semi-finals by the huns and by the same score in the first game they played in the Scottish Cup by Motherwell, at that time a team consisting of journeymen players. Legia Warsaw beat us in the first round of the Cup Winners Cup and we lost the league on that infamous last day at Ibrox. It has to be said that the only reason the league went this far before being decided was that AFC inexplicably put together an unbeaten run in the latter half of the season and the huns managed to perform in the same lacklustre and unimaginative way that the Reds had earlier in the season, producing a string of bizarre results against teams everybody expected them to beat.

The following season merely highlighted the inadequacies that had become increasingly apparent during the previous campaigns. Beaten in the Skol Cup by Airdrie, and in the Scottish Cup by the huns, AFC's European interest dies with a 3-0 defeat by a part time Danish side, BK 1903 Copenhagen. In the league, the performances and tactics were, in the main, appalling.

In early December of that year, Aberdeen were fifth in the league, lying eight points behind League leaders Hearts (aaargh!!) and five points behind the huns. They had taken just three points from a possible twelve and during November had scored just four goals, two of which were penalties and one of which was an own goal. Smith insulted the supporters by uttering the time honoured words, "Someone will soon be on the end of a real doing from us." Naturally, the famous "Boycott Pittodrie" posters appeared round the town and every game ended with a weary trudge round to the main entrance in an attempt to let this fool and the men who employed him know that enough was enough. Gerry McNee, by the way, suggested that this become a police matter and that the hooligans be severely dealt with, as did the local press, who should at least have been close enough to the supporters to realise that this was a widespread sentiment and not the action of a few militants. Not for the first or last time they preferred to churn out the Pittodrie line.

Smith was stubborn enough to remain until even our dithering Board saw the obvious and he became the first manager AFC have ever sacked, at least overtly, on February 10, 1992. Yet still he haunts us. Because the odious beings in the press think highly of him, whenever that ugly beast called crisis looks like appearing at Pittodrie, he is the source of nonsense headlines about AFC fans expecting far too much. From my limited source of stirred and twisted metaphors, I would suggest that only this man could aim lower than a snake's arse and succeed so eminently in making a pig's lug from a silken coin holder.

Such was the atmosphere when Willie Miller, who had been quietly working away in the background, was appointed as manager. His appointment has often been described as the fans' choice and it's true that some fans wanted him in the job. What greater contrast to the man who had gone before, and didn't Willie always tell it like it was; wasn't he hard as nails; didn't he have the inspirational qualities required of a manager?

The tide of reality-escaping emotion had begun, based on experience gained in a different position, taking with it a Board who seemed unable to assess the situation with the degree of dispassion necessary in a body with strategic interests and the huge responsi-

59

bility of turning around a club that was in decline. Many fans had dark forebodings, though and wondered why Willie didn't take, or wasn't forced by the Board to explore, however much his pride might have been hurt, the opportunities he'd had to learn the trade of football management away from the scene of his greatest glories.

The fanzine 'The Northern Light' described his appointment as "an easy option". Another contributor scribed the chillingly prescient words "this fanzine did not campaign to have Miller appointed and we all have reservations about what will happen." Aye, and they weren't alone.

For the remaining games of the season, Aberdeen did seem to adopt a much more adventurous style of play and, although they finished the league in fifth position, there seemed to be hope for the future. The lethargy that seemed such an innate part of the team in previous seasons looked to have departed and the players looked fit and eager. Season 1992-93, Miller's first complete season in charge, dawned, like most do for supporters, with more optimism than reality, and, although the team reached the finals of both the Skol Cup and the Scottish Cup, (and were beaten in both by the huns), league form was again erratic and we ended up runners up to the Govan thugs by a margin of nine points. Although the team played very well on occasion, it seemed that self belief often waned when most required. The much-vaunted passing game was quickly becoming mythical and desperate punts into the opposing half of the park became an increasing feature of the Dons play. All was not lost, though, and most supporters felt that with a little luck and more consistency, trophies were at least within our grasp, although it was obvious that the team did not possess the degree of skill, commitment and confidence needed to be a top class side.

The following season, 93/94, was, I believe, the most important in Miller's reign. Nearly everyone felt it was make-or-break time, and I'm sure that Willie felt the same. His frustration became more and more apparent as the season wore on and comments about competing with the huns featured ever more loudly in his chats with the gentlemen of the press. He was, entirely correctly at that point in time, equally verbose about the negative qualities of opposing teams. Although the end of the season saw us runners up to the huns by three points, Miller's frustration had become very obvious. He made numerous comments suggesting that AFC needed to change their way of thinking if they were to challenge the Govan millionaires, including the need to stop thinking as if we could never compete and to use every method possible to raise the money needed to buy players who could help the team win trophies. He felt this was needed in addition to a first class youth setup. Keen observers could sense that tension between the Board and manager was playing an increasingly prominent part in their relationship.

By the start of the 94/95 season, Willie had obviously decided that merely serving up the same fare as in previous years was not enough. Several of the more established players were allowed to leave, including Lee Richardson and Alex McLeish, and he brought in players who he felt could change things around, such as club record buy Billy Dodds. He bought Dodds despite having Scott Booth, Duncan Shearer, Eoin Jess and Joe Miller who could all play in forward positions. Still, it was remarkable that the Board had listened to the pleas for more cash, despite the oft-repeated lectures on the importance of parsimony. A left back, Woodthorpe, was also purchased, the first natural left back to play for AFC since "Beano" Robertson had left about four years previously and Hetherston, a replacement for the much-loved Richardson, was drafted into midfield. Obviously, not all of these players could play in the same game and this resulted in some of them playing in unfamiliar roles and several finding themselves dropped as seemingly second best.

He also experimented with different formations, including the infamous five at the back line up which he astonishingly called an attacking strategy. It was obvious early in the season that things were desperate, especially when they drew with Falkirk in an appalling display which caused one part of the normally sycophantic local press to be very critical. This infrequent honesty was rewarded in the way that criticism has long been dealt with at Pittodrie. Denial, anger and an incredible ability to ignore the obvious. Drew Jarvie angrily asserted that the report was rubbish in an acrimonious telephone exchange with the journalist concerned, Jim Dolan. Comments from Pittodrie quickly stopped when it became apparent that the readers of the P & J agreed with Dolan's comments. This was public confirmation of what has been felt by most of us for a very long time, namely that

61

the club has very little knowledge of the way the normal fan feels, and seems to care even less.

Very quickly after the Falkirk game came the dreadful defeat by Skonto Riga, which should have alerted everybody to how awful things had become. From this very low point the season got worse, with some incredibly awful performances and very poor results. It was as if the players didn't know one another and preferred to blame each other. Stewart McKimmie was disciplined at one stage for continuing a long-running feud with any spectator who cared to call out the odd encouraging remark. Rumours of players asking for transfers became rife, although the only ones reported in the press were Joe Miller, who went out of favour with incredible rapidity and Peter Hetherston who played very few games under Willie's guidance.

There was little consistency in team selection, even allowing for the astonishing number of injuries suffered. For the committed supporter, life had become very difficult, as the spectre of relegation began to haunt the club. Watching the team became increasingly painful. I usually had the feeling of unreality you get when feeling ill. You know that the people you are watching are the same as before but they seem so detached, so inept, so unlike their former selves, so wraithlike (The Stepford Soccer Players?)

There were numerous articles and conversations on the radio alleging that the players had stopped playing for Miller, that he'd "lost the dressing room." It certainly looked like it. AFC had become a joke. Supporters of other teams, and most of the press, were enjoying our sustained failure.

Miller compounded his mistakes by excuses which would have been unbelievable if uttered by his predecessor. That they were said by someone whose integrity had been immaculate as a player only increased his distance from the fans. The risks Miller felt it was necessary to take had, in the space of one season, become the cause of his downfall.

Eventually, he was sacked on the aforementioned dark day, leaving caretaker manager Roy Aitken only twelve games to save the team from relegation for the first time in its history. It is to his credit that Miller did not repeat the words uttered by a foreign coach in the same situation. "Why do I get the sack when it's the players who make the mistakes?" I hoped at the time that this meant that he had some insight into his shortcomings, as the easiest thing to do in his position would have been to blame the players, who undoubtedly should examine their contribution under Miller very carefully. Sadly, as late as the second last game of the season, Miller was still claiming that the club would have been safe in his hands and seemed unaware that he, at the very least, had played a part in the chaos that was now AFC.

But is it right, as some would claim, that it was all Miller's fault? The actions of the Board throughout the last few years demand some attention. To those of us who felt that Willie was the wrong appointment in the first place, the more quickly he was relieved of the managerial responsibility the better. From my point of view, as stated earlier, it was preferable to preserve the great man's reputation by taking action early rather than risk the humiliation that he was eventually to suffer.

The others who felt Willie should stay no matter what, continued to chant his name and would brook no argument that he might be part of the problem, preferring instead to snipe at the Board and reiterate the excuses Willie gave for the abysmal displays of the team. When he was eventually sacked, with precious little time for his successor to rescue us from the depths of Division One, the Board somehow contrived to alienate both those who wished Willie to be sacked earlier in the season and those who felt he should continue. While there is no doubt that the nature and timing of the decision to sack Willie was difficult and was bound to upset some, it still takes an awful lot to alienate nearly all the AFC support. To try to deflect the criticism by announcing a share issue almost immediately is nothing short of contemptible, however worthy an idea you think it might be.

The cynical might suggest that the reason Willie was described as the fans' choice, the reason he got the job in the first place, was so that the Board would never have to endure the criticism and torment they received when Alex Smith was gradually steering the club down the toilet. What better way to ensure that didn't happen than to employ one of the club's biggest heroes? At least that way if things go awry you can say, "We listened to the fans and made our judgement accordingly." I don't want to believe that this is what happened but it's certainly a possibility. If so, then I hope a thousand giant hornets become stuck in the collective underpants of the Board and that their huge, corporate, wrinkled arse gets stung with appropriate venom.

On the other hand, maybe they just let the emotion that every Reds' fan feels for Willie get the better of their judgement. If that's the case, they are guilty of the same offence as at least one section of the support. I'd hoped for better than that from a group trying to make rational, strategic decisions. It was wrong to put Willie in that position, however much we all wanted him to succeed. His pride would have demanded he take the job and it's unlikely that he would ever express any doubts about his own ability, which in truth needed development, either within the club in a different role or away from Pittodrie for a couple of years. These actions have meant that our finest ever player is left with a bitterness for some at the club, even though he'll probably remain as a supporter. This is so, so sad, and worse, it was preventable.

Perhaps the traumas of the 94/95 season will allow everyone associated with Aberdeen Football Club, be they fans, players, management or directors to take stock, to learn from their mistakes and to listen to each other's opinions without rancour and blame. We must do everything we can to make sure that the icon that we all worship, AFC, does not suffer because of reliance on emotion or lack of common purpose.

And if in the future a player ever shows the same loyalty to the club as Willie Miller has done, let's handle it properly and allow everyone to retain some dignity. If you're a fan, that means not immediately demanding that he becomes manager if the person in charge at the time happens to be a complete buffoon. If you're a director, it means being cruel to be kind, and not appointing him as manager until he has proved himself elsewhere. We can ignore, perhaps, the taunts of others who love to see us fail. We can't afford to alienate our greatest heroes by placing them on an emotional pedestal that is bound to collapse under the weight of reality and inexperience.

Heroes and Villains

The boys look great in training. Sound familiar? If this comment, frequently offered from the Pittodrie staff, were to be believed then it's a pity that the Scottish League didn't schedule our games for 10:30 am. Monday to Friday.

For all the trauma behind the scenes, the guys who produced 31 games of thud and blunder before realising that their proverbial arses were edging ever closer to the outside of the tent must be held accountable. Sure, in the end we saw more entertainment

66

in the last 450 minutes of the season than we had done in the previous three years, but we can't forget what had gone before and the players who played a major part in putting us there.

Theo Snelders - The flying Dutchman was 'hoot' injured and even suspended for a large chunk of the season. When he did play his form was patchy, either making stunning saves from Stench or letting trundlers from Keith Wright beat him via his scrotum.

5/10

Stephen Wright - HUN!!!!!.

0/10

Stewart McKimmie - The Terminator struck up a unique rapport with the South Stand faithful. His one-pronged assault caused some of them to lose their travelling rugs and choke on the contents of their (un)hip flasks. His on-field activities were less exciting. If he passes water with the same accuracy as he passes a football his bathroom floor must be swimming in pish. As a captain, his communication technique resembles Helen Keller's and his motivational qualities are pure John Major. His improved form towards the end of the season masked the fact that for Stewarty it was a gey naff season.

3/10

Gary Smith - Three years ago Smiffy was being compared favourably to a young Willie Miller. Last season he was held in the same esteem as Bertie Miller. He was caught in more compromising positions than Hugh Grant and was beaten more times than a Tory MP at an S & M party. A return to form is a necessity next season

3/10

Brian Irvine - What can I add about Dobbin that you all don't know already? Cut the man in half and you'd end with a bloody mess on the floor and we'd be short of a centre half. Some say that he'd have Aberdeen written right through him. I would be very surprised. However, there's no doubt that he cares about the club and the fans and always gives 100%. Willie seemed ready to send him to the knacker's yard, yet when Roy brought him back he scored a stunner against Celtic, played an inch-perfect 50-yard ball to Shearer for the third goal in the Dunfermline game at Pittodrie and his defending was awesome. The only mistake Dobbin made in the last few games was to kiss his Umbro badge instead of the club badge after the first leg of the play-offs. Big Roy will prefer Inglis at his peril next season.

8/10

Brian Grant - Granty played as well last season as he did the season before.

3/10

Paul Kane - Not a bonny loon but a fine loon. Apparently does 'a lot of work for charidee mate'. Unfortunately a lot of this charity work came between the hours of 3 pm. and 4:45 pm. every Saturday. Despite his poor form he didn't deserve to be booed during the Hibs game.

3/10

Ray McKinnon - As Evan Dando put it, 'It's a shame about Ray'. The Raymeister is a talented loon but seems to have his mind more on the 3:15 at Catterick than the 3:00 at Pittodrie. Appears not to like it up him.

3/10

Peter Hetherston - The Silkster and Willie didn't seem to hit it off, which makes you wonder why Willie signed him in the first place. Did the business late on with some good performances, particularly against the pass-backs. Mrs. Silky doesn't seem to think much of Aberdeen as she's moved back to Coatbridge!! Each to their own I suppose, but Silky may find himself in a difficult club v. old lady battle.

7/10

Eoin Jess - What is it with Eoin? He's got more talent than a pub full of Supermodels yet still only turns in a couple of decent performances a season. Stated at the start of the season that he wanted to play like Peter Beardsley but the closest he got was to have his hair cut like Peter Beardsley.

4/10

Joe Miller - Joe put away his catty and sweeties of old and became a man amongst boys with his best ever season, well, half season, as Willie didn't fancy Joe much either. (Anyone see a trend developing?). His performance against Falkirk was stunning and his goal against Dunfermline long overdue. Sparky's player of the season

9/10

Duncan Shearer - His goal against the Huns when he dispossessed McCall. The goal against the Arabs, first-timed past O'Hanlon. The third against Dunfermline, taking a Dobbin through ball in his stride and smashing it past Van De Kamp.

"It's a goal Duncan Shearer, it's a goal Duncan Shearer, walking along, singing a song, walking in a Shearer wonderland" Enough said.

7/10

Billy Dodds - The jury is still out on Doddsy, he almost made missing sitters an art form, but still managed six goals in six games when the pressure was at its most intense. Perhaps now that he's played in a team that hasn't been relegated he'll more relaxed next season. Hopefully the T-shirt of King Joey that he wore in the last few games will become a permanent fixture.

6/10

Stephen Glass - I have seen the future and it is Glass. The best thing to come out of Dundee since the A90 provided Dundonians with an escape route.

8/10

John Inglis - Willie's last signing already had the respect of the Pittodrie faithful for nicking David Murray's bird, allegedly. Despite being our centre-half he managed to score more league goals than Ray McKinnon and Joe Miller and as many as Eoin Jess.

5/10

Colin Woodthorpe - Our first natural left-back since Beano. Looked good going forward but not so good defending. May have been a victim of Willie's 3-5-2/5-3-2 debacle. Didn't fill his nostrils with the sweet smell of success too often, was only on the winning side three times.

4/10

Scott Booth - If the rumours about Scott were to be believed during last season he had a hip injury, nervous breakdown, cancer, AIDS, bubonic plague, yellow fever, scarlet fever and cup fever. There were those who say there was nothing wrong at all. Whatever, during the few games he did play he scored nine goals which made him third top scorer. He is without doubt a valuable asset and up to the point of his injury, whilst playing for Scotland, was our most effective player. Haste ye back.

8/10

Hugh Robertson - Shug scored two goals in two games at the start of the season and was then 'rested'. He must have been fucking knackered 'cos he was hardly seen for the rest of the season. Looked the part in the six games he was fit enough to play. Deserves a starting place next season.

7/10

Scott Thomson - Nipper did enough during the season to show that he has the ability to become a regular. After scoring against Falkirk you could see his confidence rise. Rumours of laziness in training abound. If his attitude is right he'll make his mark

5/10

David Winnie - FUCK OFF!!!!!!!

-10/10

Statistics and Records 1994/95

APPEARANCES

Most (All matches)   .... Billy Dodds (43)

GOALS

Top Scorer (All matches)   .... Billy Dodds (16)

Top Scorer (Premier League)   .... Billy Dodds (14)

Top Scorer (Scottish Cup)   .... Eoin Jess (1)

Top Scorer (Paul McStay Cup)   .... Duncan Shearer (4)

Top Scorer (UEFA Cup)   .... Paul Kane (1)

Top Scorer (Premier Play-offs)   .... Duncan Shearer (2)
                                     .... Stephen Glass   (2)

STRIKE RATES (goals per starting appearances)

Scott Booth............................... 9 goals in 14 games (64.3%)

Billy Dodds.............................. 16 goals in 44 games (36.4%)

Eoin Jess.................................. 2 goals in 18 games (11.1%)

Duncan Shearer........................ 13 goals in 25 games (52.0%)

GOALKEEPERS' RECORDS
(clean sheets per starting appearances)

Theo Snelders..................................... 13 in 33 games (39.4%)

Michael Watt.. 2 in 13 games (15.4%)
(note: no cheap jokes about Michael having kept clean sheets on
his recent honeymoon)

Right, that's the obligatory boring statistical bit out of the way, anoraks. The season's **real** stats and records are listed below. Expect none of these in Rothman's 1996 volume.

GOAL OF THE SEASON
(TRF contributors' choices)

Bloo Toon	*Shearer's 2nd v*		*Dunfermline 21 May*	
OBE	*Irvine*	*v*	*Celtic*	*15 April**
Sparky	*Shearer's 2nd v*		*Dunfermline 21 May*	
M. Standing	*Shearer*	*v*	*the Huns*	*12 Feb.*
The Count	*Shearer*	*v*	*United*	*6 May*
Uncle Albert	*Irvine*	*v*	*Celtic*	*15April**
Gordon Reid	*Shearer*	*v*	*United*	*6 May*
Niall	*Irvine*	*v*	*Celtic*	*15 April**

*Described by Gordon Reid as "Well worthy of the Golden Horseshoe".

Footnote: There were a number of mentions of Stephen Wright's 50 yarder against the Jags (11 March), but since the scorer's now joined the Brothers of Beelzebub, it's been withdrawn from nominations. Looking at it now, in the cool light of day, it was a flukey effort from the most overrated right back the Huns have ever signed from us in July 1995. Fair enough?

PLAYER OF THE SEASON
(TRF contributors' choices)

Bloo Toon	*Billy Dodds*
Old Beach Ender	*(Doesn't believe in this)*
Sparky	*Joe Miller*
Mainly Standing	*Stephen Glass*
The Count	*Brian Irvine*
Uncle Albert	*Stephen Glass*
Gordon Reid	*Brian Irvine*
Niall	*Brian Irvine*

CARETAKER MANAGER OF THE SEASON

NEW RECORDS SET DURING 1994/95

Highest aggregate number of pints sunk by fanzine staff

The Red Final. 6 May following the Dundee United game. Venues: The Blue Lamp, The City Bar and some forgotten curry house visited by Sparky. Total: Very vague.........

Furthest sprint by ageing amateur hacks carrying the Flossie banner

Mainly Standing and The Count. 25 May following the Play-off 2nd leg. Venue: East End Park. Distance: The halfway line to find the asshole waving the Union Jack.

Gob of the season

A certain Northsound Radio DJ (the offending projectile was green, this may provide you with a clue). 2nd June. Venue: All over Stench Hateley, the lavvy, the Paramount Bar. No following wind - the record stands.

Best new songs

All Around My Hat	*(Steeleye Span arr. M. Standing)*
	Mainly Standing 1995
The Sombrero Song	*(trad. arr. Old Beach Ender)*
	Old Beach Ender 1995
Who Ate All The Pies	*(unknown, arr. TRF choir)*
	TRF Away Choir 1995
Great Escape Barmy Army	*(Great Escape Barmy Army)*
	GEBA** 1995

*** Identify yourselves guys, we'd like to do the video.*

Paid to watch the Dons!

Free buses. 11 March. Venue: Firhill. All stewards on the free buses that day were promised a ticket to get into the game. On arrival at Pittodrie on the Saturday morning, John Morgan informed them that the Jags had refused to provide tickets on request. All stewards had then to sign a document confirming that they had received a tenner from the club. There were some crap performances, but being paid to watch the merd on display is surely a first. The way we chucked away a two-goal lead that day made me wonder if they should have held out for twenty.

Faithful through and through etc.

The Celtic away support, who for years following some spankings at Pittodrie would stay behind for ages singing songs of false bravado and misplaced loyalty while the rest of us were in the boozer. 15 April. Venue: Pittodrie. Disappeared like Huns from a home defeat a long time before the end as we celebrated beating them, but still staying bottom of the League.

Penalty v Huns

Not one, but two! 24 September and 12 February. Venue: Pittodrie. Having gone the best part of what seemed like a decade without being awarded a penalty of any sort, against any side, the Masons forgot the script and awarded us penalties in successive home League games against the Huns. Billy Dodds scored both. Watch the TV replay of the one on 24 September. As Beel turns to run back to the centre circle, does he make some derogatory remark to the Stenchmeister? Looks like it to me.

No penalties for Huns

Not one but two! (This according to arch-Hun Jock ~~Blue~~ Brown). 12 February. Venue: Pittodrie. Jim McCluskey. Sorry, I'll repeat that. Jim McCluskey, yes, he of sash, bowler, white gloves, drum, flute and baton, misses two almost legitimate Hun penalty claims as Miller and Laudrup fall in the box. Gave us one on the same day! Failed to send Maxwell off though. Still, mustn't grumble..........

Topics of Conversation

At work, on the phone, at home, on public transport, the sole topic of conversation it seemed, was the then current plight of the Dons. Would they, wouldn't they avoid the insult of relegation, which itself would have been a record? There were those who claimed to be Dons' supporters who said that a season in the First Division would have done us good. Not a chance! To have been relegated would have meant disaster for the club and for those of us who follow for all the right reasons.

Most annoying were the boneheads who kept asking, "What will you do on Saturdays next season if they go down?" What a bloody stupid question. Are Aberdeen fans genetically programmed to start visiting B&Q of a Saturday afternoon just because we happen to be playing in a different division?

You just don't realise, do you?

What the record number of conversations concerning the crisis proved was that people genuinely do care despite all the cynicism and backbiting that goes on. For many, even beyond the sizeable number of loyal fanatics who would crawl naked for a thousand miles over broken glass just to watch the Pittodrie grass grow, the horror of 1994/95 was the most important aspect of their lives during that nightmare.

Not one of us ever want to have to go through that again........

...NEVER AGAIN, DO YOU HEAR?

Revival

Saturday April 1st 1995. It's approaching 4:45 and the Dons are slipping to their fourth defeat by Kilmarnock this season. Statisticians are frantically skimming the rule books to see if this means that the Ayrshire side get to keep us to stick on their mantelpiece. If Kilmarnock are the bailiffs of the Premier League then today they pinned a final notice of eviction on the front door of Pittodrie.

Despite relentlessly bombarding the Killie goalmouth we

couldn't break through, a Mark Skilling goal is enough to sink us. Relegation to the First Division, for so many years a pilgrimage reserved for the Dundees and Particks of this world, is now staring us in the face. The faithful have every right to be pissed off. However, what happened after the final whistle blew, in my humble opinion, heralded the start of the now famous revival. Despite a side containing Roger Connor and Steve Maskrey having beaten us four times in one season - even though we were six games away from biannual trips to Morton and Dumbarton - the Red Army gave the team a standing ovation. They appreciated that on this day the team had given their all without getting the merest sniff of a break.

The players, no doubt dreading another chorus of boos and the Directors, getting ready for another demo, must have been amazed and would have taken heart from this incredible response. The entire Red Army, fans and players alike, now seemed galvanised by this show of defiance. We would carry on with the same ferocity of support until the end of the season.

With twelve games to go in the most catastrophic season in the history of the club we were without a manager. This, coupled with the fact that the Huns were our next opponents, left Ian Donald with the problem of having to appoint a caretaker manager in time to lift our flagging spirits. Why Willie was sacked without any replacement being approached, without even having a replacement in mind, is beyond me but the fact was that Ian publicly stated that he didn't have a clue who was going to steer the sinking ship. Luckily for him there was a man on the staff who throughout his career has been an inspiration for all around him and was hated by the opposition, the perfect choice for lifting our flagging spirits and giving us hope of better days to come. Unfortunately Angus the Bull turned the job down when Ian refused to let him have Wee Alickie as his assistant.

Ian was forced to go down the line and ask Big Roy to do the job. There's a general rule of thumb that when a manager is sacked the backroom staff go with him, fortunately for Ian Donald, Roy Aitken was the exception to the rule.

Roy's first game in charge was at home to the Huns, a unique occasion. Many fans went to vent their spleen against a board that had ended Willie Miller's long association with the club. Others accepted the decision as a necessary evil and looked to the players to respond. The chants of 'One Willie Miller' were plentiful prior to kick-off and when the whistle blew the attitude of the players was a revelation. A penalty by Dodds and a Shearer special in the second half sent 19,000 Rudolphs delirious and gave us hope that happy days were here again. Sure, there were still chants for Willie on the way out, but they were not as vociferous as they had been at the start. The team on the park was the one that Willie had built, but they bore no resemblance to the eleven that had made us suffer so often in the preceding four months. Jess teased and tormented, Wright and Glass gave Laudrup his hardest game in a Hun shirt. Something had inspired the players, whether it was the realisation that time was running out, or relief at the change of leadership, we will probably never know.

One thing that had remained constant throughout this season of inconsistency was that if we won one week we wouldn't the next. As the next game was against Stenhousemuir in the cup, that would surely change. Thoughts of relegation were beginning to fade and dreams of a visit to Hampden for a Cup Final were beginning to germinate in more than a few Dandies' minds.

What happened at Stenhousemuir is well documented by The Count in an earlier chapter. For me, in London for the weekend, it was bad enough that whilst the game was going on at Ochilview I'd wasted £7 going to the cinema to see 'Solitaire for Two', scandalously described as 'The best British Comedy since Four Weddings..'. It was of course the only British comedy since Four Weddings, and they use the word *comedy* in the loosest possible sense. My escape from the drivel on the screen was the knowledge that 400 miles away the Dons would be signalling their return to form by cuffing Second division, fourth rate opposition. The phone call that informed me of the score was laughed off as a very poor wind-up, but the news of a major upset in the Scottish Cup on BBC2 news could not be treated as a joke.

The following Saturday was memorable only for my verbal jousting with Jim Traynor, Bob Crampsey, King Joey et al on Radio Scotland's 'Sportsound' programme. Cameron described the team as disgraceful, Crampsey thought we'd no good players and Traynor thought that we should never have sacked Smith. I tried manfully to put a brave but realistic face on things, stating that the fans were still behind the team and escape from our precarious position was not beyond us. The 2-0 defeat by Motherwell and

Theo's early bath did more for the panel's arguments than mine.

After the nation watched Pierre Van Hooydonk fall like a felled redwood after a slight collision with Dobbin, then miraculously recover to score both goals in a televised 2-0 defeat by Celtic, things looked increasingly grim. Hope was at hand, our next game was at Firhill against bottom of the league Partick Thistle. A Dons victory would almost certainly cut the Harry Wraggs adrift and leave us battling with three or four others to avoid the play-off spot. The game was so important that the Board laid on free buses to ferry fans to the match. The Glasgow press took the opportunity to dream up hilarious stories about the buses being used by Aberdeen shoppers too tight to pay the normal fare to Glasgow. I laughed until I stopped.

I didn't go to the game, though in hindsight this was a grave error. I spent the afternoon in the car going through the agonies of listening to regular updates from Radio Scotland. At one stage I'd made the mistake of listening to Radio Clyde and heard Chic 'Shagger' Young saying that Aberdeen fans would have to get used to the fact that Kilmarnock are a bigger club than we are! The fact that the car radio was my only link with Firhill saved me from putting my fist through it. Instead I made a mental note that if I ever met the wee Hun I'd kick the shit out of him.

Back to Radio Scotland, about 3:15 I'm sitting at the lights at the Bridge of Don when news of Stephen Wright's goal comes through. There is no more agonising moment known to man than those two seconds between Richard Gordon saying, "There's been a goal at Firhill" and the reporter telling you who the goal is for. In that short space of time you try to analyse all available data to give you a clue. The tone of Richard Gordon's voice, the sound of the crowd in the background, anything that gives you an idea of what the reporter is about to say.

On this occasion, it was Stephen Wright's goal from the halfway line. Things were looking good. Before half-time Billy Dodds had added a second. Things were looking decidedly rosy. I let my guard drop, I relaxed, safe in the knowledge that the three points were ours and a major step to Premier League safety was about to be taken. I should have known better, a goal early in the second half by Pitman was ominous and it was no surprise when news of Tommy Turner's equaliser came through. The only surprise was how I didn't crash while driving and banging my head off the steering wheel at the same time. I ended up almost glad that we hung on for a 2-2 draw. It seemed evident that the Dons had forgotten how to win. It didn't help that on the same day Hibs did what we had failed to do, by gubbing Stenhousemuir.

A 0-0 draw at home to Hibs offered some encouragement. There was more fight about the team, and if it hadn't been for Jim Leighton putting in the kind of display he regularly made for us, we would have won doing handstands. We were helped by the fact that Hibs looked as if they needed an ordnance survey map and a compass to find our box. A draw was of little use though, wins were what we needed, but there were stirrings of better things to come.

The following week was the Kilmarnock game described at the start of the chapter. I can't stress enough how important the show of defiance by the fans at the end of that game was.

Kilmarnock had come looking for a draw but, thanks to Lekjovic's brilliance, some woeful finishing and some downright bad luck, picked up all three. I'm convinced that had Big Roy thrown on Brian Irvine up front for the last twenty minutes we'd have won the game. We must have forced a dozen corners in that period without really looking like scoring from one. Big Dobbin would have changed all that. We lost but the fans appreciated the efforts. If they had gone the other way, booed the team off the pitch and demonstrated in Pittodrie Street I feel sure we would be in Division One next season. The players knew, if they hadn't before, that the fans would follow them everywhere. If we were going down we were all going down together.

We took up our full ticket allocation from the Huns for the trip to Iprix. I know that a full allocation from the Huns only comes to about thirty tickets, but it was important that they were all snapped up. I couldn't go and kept up with the match in a way even more stressful than waiting for updates on Radio Scotland - I was glued to teletext. When, within the first twenty minutes, the Huns had scored twice I gave up and watched the agonies of my horse coming second in the Grand National. Not my day really. After the race I cautiously put the text back on in trepidation as to what score might be facing me. 2-2! I couldn't believe it, Dodds and Shearer had brought us back into the game. In the second half disaster struck when the teletext went on the blink.

It's bad enough waiting for scores to update on teletext but knowing that they **can't** update is torture. By the time I'd sussed out something was wrong, Stench had scored the third and we'd gone down bravely. I still tried to be positive. We'd come back from 2-0 and would have been 3-2 in front had Paul Kane's perfectly good goal been allowed to stand. Results elsewhere, particularly Dundee United's poor run meant that there was still hope.

Defeat by Celtic on April 25th would have left us on a one-way trip up shit creek not only paddle-free but without a canoe. Partick had gone on a winning streak that beggared belief and we couldn't really expect Dundee United to lose every game, could we? There was no real reason to be optimistic, since, save for the win in his first game, Roy's managerial record was unblemished by victory. The game was notable for the return of Brian Irvine, just the kind of 100% trier we needed at this time. Fortunately Celtic were a poor side. When Duncan Shearer nodded us in front the result was never in doubt. Dobbin's magnificent second just before half time helped us to relax and enjoy the second half. We still needed to win our last four games, but with the support fully behind the team, that was possible. Next stop was Motherwell on Tuesday night.

Somewhere between 2,500-3,500 Rudolphs made their way to Fir Park that Tuesday night. It was the night that Charlie Allan ate all the pies, as documented in TRF 12. This was also the night that, for the first and only time, I was sure we were going down. Motherwell took the lead through Sean McSkimming but Billy Dodds quickly equalised. Despite the brave efforts of Michael Watt, Dougie Arnott put Motherwell in front and they then survived twenty minutes of constant Dons' pressure. Irvine and Glass hit the upright but Motherwell hung on. The irony of what may have been the final nail in our coffin being driven in by a side managed by Big Red was not lost on me. Worse than the score at Fir Park was that Dundee United had beaten Partick Thistle 3-1. We were now cut adrift from the rest of the league by four points with only three games to go.

The largest municipal toilet in Scotland, Tynecastle, beckoned. Another huge Red Army was there to watch what truly was a make or break game. If we lost and Dundee United beat Hibs we were relegated.

The Bloo Toon express arrived in Edinburgh at about 12:30. The first task was to find a pub with some friendly faces in it. Unfortunately we decided to follow my directions and walked in a circle for about fifteen minutes before landing in a pub filled with

Dandies directly across from the ground. The pub was jumping and the atmosphere was superb. Song after song, drink after drink flowed. By the time we left to go to the match I was convinced that defeat was not on the menu.

Inside the ground the Red Army made the best of the shitty conditions we were seated in. The game was one of the tensest I've ever encountered in my days following the Dons. Hearts missed early chances through Hamilton and Colquhoun. Gradually, as half time approached, we were in the ascendancy, but still no goals. News filtered through that Gordan Petric had been sent off at Tannadice, which meant that United would be missing four of their star players for the Pittodrie showdown and the mood amongst the Dons' fans grew increasingly optimistic. Into the second half Shearer was bundled over by Hagen. Penalty! I couldn't look, Old Beach Ender managed to peek through his fingers as Billy Dodds stroked the ball to his left with Nelson going the wrong way. 1-0. The celebrations were unprecedented, *we're shite but we're staying up.*

Five minutes later, Hen McPherson nodded in an equaliser, played onside by Joe Miller, slow coming off the post at a corner. Now the fingernails are thoroughly chewed to the bone, so I borrowed OBE's. The next twenty minutes were torture, we huffed and we puffed but didn't look like knocking Hearts down. Five minutes to go, Brian Grant floated in a cross from the right, Dodds escaped his marker and glanced it into the same corner as the penalty had nestled twenty minutes earlier. Chaos ensued. The Red Final contingent formed one collective bundle of hugging humanity.

The Count, with his referee's head on, noticed that Dodds, already booked, could be sent off for running to the crowd to celebrate. Fortunately the ref. acted sensibly and allowed Dodds his moment of glory. The final five minutes were torture, the Dons defended resolutely and Shearer almost scored a third. When the final whistle went there was a huge cheer from the Red Army, half of it in delight at the victory, the other half in relief that the season was still alive. Within seconds the cheers increased as news of Pat McGinlay scoring the only goal of the game at Tannadice filtered through. Dundee United would be coming to Pittodrie the following week only a point ahead and without McKinlay, Welsh, Bowman and Petric who were all suspended.

Gorgie Road has never looked so beautiful. Sure it still smelled like Mark Hateley's jockstrap but the sight of 4,000 Rudolphs singing in the street was wonderful. "All Around My Hat", the Count and Mainly Standing anthem, was sung continuously, interspersed only with a song warning of the dangers of being in the company of Elton John?! As the Bloo Toon glory train pulled out of Edinburgh we wound down the windows informing anyone and everyone that it was "2-1 to the Aberdeen". We were two wins away from at least the play-offs.

The build-up to the United game was unlike any other league game I can remember. The only topic of conversation in town that week was the game. Did you have a ticket? Could you get me a ticket? All the mathematical possibilities were calculated and recalculated. It was simple, well fairly simple. If Aberdeen won they'd only need a draw at Falkirk on the last day to ensure at least a play-off slot. If it was a draw, United would need to win on the last day, or if Aberdeen didn't beat Falkirk a draw on the last day would keep United up. If United won we were relegated. Ninety minutes stood between us and First Division football.

The media circus was in full swing, OBE and I were on Radio Five Live, The Count and Mainly Standing were on Northsound and even Charlie Allan was on Sky Sports, widescreen of course. On the day of the game, I was in the comfy seats in the Dick End with a free bar available from 2:00. Win, lose or draw the bar would be well used - to calm nerves, celebrate or drown sorrows. The atmosphere inside Pittodrie was unbelievable. Everyone, apart from most of the people in the seats beside me, was in full voice.

The game itself was a fairly nervy affair. With half-time approaching, Joe Miller made a great break down the right, his cross was met at full tilt by Jess whose header was palmed out to Billy Dodds who poked it in. A subtle mix of euphoria, relief and lager sends me dancing along the walkway in front of my seat, hugging and high-fiving anybody within reach. At half-time we hurried back to the hospitality lounge in order to secure our free pies, just in case Charlie Allan was lurking in the vicinity.

When the whistle blew for the second half I was one of the only ones sitting in the comfy seats. Whilst the hospitality laid on at half-time is very tasty I can't see how it can be a greater attraction than the most important 45 minutes ever played at Pittodrie. Corporate entertainment is here to stay. I just wished that on this day it had been taken up by those who really cared about the result, not those who had to check their complimentary team sheets when Duncan Shearer or Eoin Jess had the ball.

The second half was ferocious. Christian Dailly dished out some distinctly un-Christian tackles on Stephen Wright and Eoin Jess. The Dons' second goal was sheer poetry. Midway through the second half Joe Miller played the ball inside to Silky who turned away from his marker, played a tremendous ball to Billy Dodds, who in turn laid it into the path of Duncan Shearer. Taking it in his stride, Duncan drilled it first time past O'Hanlon.

It's a goal Duncan Shearer, it's a goal Duncan Shearer, we're walking along singing a song, walking in a Shearer wonderland.

Once again the genius that is Duncan Shearer had secured the game for the Dons, well almost. There was a slight hiccup when United scored five minutes from time, but it was merely a consolation. Easy to say that now, but that five minutes were probably the longest I can remember at Pittodrie, certainly the most nail-biting since the Bayern Munich game in 1983.

We survived and were now in the position where a draw would secure at least a play-off slot. The team that only six weeks previously were playing with the poetic grace of McGonagall had transformed into a team of Lord Byrons (not the pub) and we were all waxing lyrical about our survival chances.

That night Aberdeen was the place to be. The Red Final boys had arranged to meet Neil McDougall in the Blue Lamp as we thought it would be fairly quiet. In hindsight this was not one of the best laid plans of sheep and men. The Blue Lamp was jumping, Dandies everywhere drinking a toast to survival. Everyone was in full voice, and every song sung at Pittodrie during the last thirty years got a rendition. Henning Boel, Davie Robb, King Joey and Jim Forrest all got a mention. A group of Dandies who were obviously related to Pans People hailed themselves the Great Escape Barmy Army and had actions to match the song. The City Bar Reds joined in the merrymaking and before long we made our way down to the City Bar itself, where The Count, Mainly Standing and myself quaffed a few more flagons of ale with the CBRs. An unforgettable night was had by all, except for me. I couldn't remember much about it the next day although most of it has come back to me in glorious flashbacks since.

Our final regular season game saw us travelling to Falkirk. A trip to Brockville is usually looked forward to with the same relish as a turkey looks forward to Christmas. The ground is a toilet, speaking of which the toilet in the home end holds about six people at a push. God knows what you do if you're a woman. The Grill has better female toilet facilities.

Earlier in the season it had taken us thirty minutes to get in through the two turnstiles at the visitors' end. With 8,000 of us set to travel this time it was thought that overnight accommodation would be required if we wanted to get for the kick-off.

On arriving in Falkirk at around midday the first thing we saw was a group of Huns getting ready for the trip to Iprix. This sight was repeated throughout the town which confirmed my suspicions that Falkirk fans are, in the main, Huns in disguise.

There was much talk after the game about Dons' fans running riot throughout the town. I for one didn't see any trouble. The Rudolphs that were in the Behind the Wall pub were all well behaved and even stopped singing when the bouncer told them to. I'm sure that there was no more trouble than when the old firm visit but the Glasgow press, obviously pissed off that we took a greater travelling support with us than either the Huns or the Tims, had to make out that we were all hooligans intent on causing trouble.

The game itself was not a classic, the shit condition of the pitch coupled with the lack of talent in the Falkirk side saw to that, but the enormous Dons' support didn't care. The 2-0 win was memorable for the fact that it assured us of at least a place in the play-offs and marked the first goals in the first team for both Scott Thomson and Stephen Glass. When it was announced that Hearts had beaten Motherwell, it confirmed our place in the play-offs. This result sent Falkirk fans into wild delight. Obviously they have great empathy with the Jambos as they are also Huns that can't afford the fare to Govan. The wild jubilation of the Falkirk fans ensured that I'll look forward to gubbing them in all four encounters next season and take great delight at watching them struggle for Premier League survival.

The news of the Hearts' score left me with a strange feeling. I was delighted that we'd won but I'd fully expected Big Red's boys to do us a favour by beating the Jambos thus ensuring survival without the need for a play-off. I didn't worry too much, the way we were playing, the play-off would be a formality.

Back in the car we discovered that Raith had drawn 0-0 which gave them the First Division title and ensured that Dunfermline would be our opponents in the first play-off in Scottish football history.

The buildup to the first leg of the play-off was completely different to the Dundee United game. There was definitely a feeling that the hard work had been done and that Dunfermline would be lambs to the slaughter. Tickets were, again, sold out although, unlike the United game they took until the Thursday afternoon to go, perhaps a sign that many people thought it was a foregone conclusion.

On the day of the game I strolled down King Street confident that I was about to witness the Dons winning by three goals. I arrived at the ground at 2:00 to meet the Count and OBE selling the last of the TRF 12. OBE was tense, pointing out the difference in atmosphere from the United game. My assurances that the game was as good as won fell on deaf ears as OBE continually muttered about over confidence. Even my assertions that any team with Norrie McCathie and Craig Robertson playing hadn't a hope of winning at Pittodrie were scoffed at.

Inside the ground John McRuvie did his customary excellent job of getting the fans going by announcing that Willie was in the crowd. Cue cries of "One Willie Miller, there's only one Willie Miller" although I didn't think the cries were as passionate as they were at the Hun game directly after Willie's sacking. Then John informed us that Lee Richardson was in the crowd, the Dick End erupted into the traditional 'Oh oh Rico, oh oh Rico' chant, accompanied by the necessary bowing and scraping. Rumour has it that Rico was actually walking down Merkland Road at the time, but no matter, it got the crowd singing.

As the game crawled towards half-time my confidence began to falter, thoughts of spending the TRF postmortem listening to OBE saying, "I told you so" began to fill my head. Then Stephen Glass caressed a left-footed free-kick into the bottom corner of Van De Kamp's goal. Relief, an emotion that was getting all too familiar, swept over Pittodrie We could now sit back and enjoy the barrow-load of goals that would doubtless follow. Wrong. Early in the second half the lumberjack Craig Robertson headed Dunfermline level then stood in a crouched pose waving his fists at the Dick

End, looking not unlike a constipated grizzly bear making one last effort to squeeze out a log that has been building up for a week.

There is a bright side to everything though. As Robertson was performing his rendition of the Maori Haka in our goalmouth, the guy behind me came away with one of the best quips I'd heard all season.

"Fat bastard, think I'll send him a death threat". Who says there's no humour at Pittodrie?

There was definitely an uneasy feeling around the ground. Dunfermline's time-wasting tactics were going unpunished by Buster Mottram. Within five minutes of the equaliser though, we were back in front. Who else but Duncan Shearer heading us in front from a nice cut-back by Stewart McKimmie, honest!

Most people inside the ground realised that a one goal lead would give Dunfermline some hope of getting a result at East End Park. A two goal lead would shut the door in their faces.

Stephen Glass produced the finest individual piece of skill seen at Pittodrie for many a season. Picking the ball up inside his own half, he waltzed round four Dunfermline defenders, then with only the keeper to beat he hit it over the bar. It would have been goal of the season, and if Laudrup had done it, Gerry McKnee-jerk would have been verbally masturbating over it for months.

With a couple of minutes left Brian Irvine played an exquisite through ball which beat the Dunfermline offside trap. Duncan ran on to it, took one touch to set the ball up, then drilled a magnificent shot on the drop past the helpless Van De Kamp. It was a brilliant goal and one that I'm sure no-one inside the ground, except for a few Pars fans, will ever forget.

From then until the end of the game all Dons' fans in the ground were united in constant renditions of the "It's a goal Duncan Shearer" anthem.

By the way the two teams left the park you could sense that the tie was over. Dunfermline trudged off the park, heads bowed, knowing that a goal deficit was at least one too many. The Dons marched off saluting the fans, happy in the knowledge that, in their present form, the best of sides would have difficulty pulling back two goals. One more highlight followed. Brian Irvine ran off the pitch kissing his badge, except he kissed the wrong side and pledged his allegiance to Umbro. Still we knew what he meant.

Outside the ground a large queue formed for tickets for the

away leg, a sign that despite the Dons looking home and dry the faithful Reds weren't going to miss the writing of the final chapter to this bizarre season.

The premature celebrations went on long into the night. As I stood at the Art Gallery at 7:30, awaiting Mrs. Sparky picking me up, I could hear, drifting gently in the breeze the anthem "It's a goal Duncan Shearer...". If I had a custard cream for every time that song was sung that day I'd have an awful lot of biscuits.

In the week leading up to the second leg, Dunfermline's manager Bert Paton and various players spewed forth in the press about how they fancied their chances as they had shown in the game at Pittodrie that they were as good as Aberdeen. Check the score losers.

I was dealt a hammer blow when I discovered that I was expected in London on business on Wednesday and Thursday which meant that I'd miss the game. I took the precaution of reserving one of OBE's spare tickets, just in case I managed to pull off an escape act on a par with The Dons.

On arriving in London it turned out that, due to various circumstances, my two day jaunt was only to take half a day, leaving me free to join the Red Army on manoeuvres to Dunfermline. It was definitely an omen, I was meant to be there to see us survive.

Every silver lining has its cloud. It was my turn to drive. The Sparky glory train pulled into Dunfermline at 6:00 allowing Bloo Toon and his comrade-in-arms Mike plenty of time to get tanked up whilst I sampled the local coke, Coca-Cola that is. We journeyed to the ground by taxi, well almost. The driver was ready to dump us after Bloo Toon claimed that his route to the ground wasn't the most direct. I didn't realise that Bloo Toon was an expert on all roads to East End Park. It transpired that Bloo Toon was speaking pish and after smoothing things over with the driver we arrived at the ground. We immediately met in with Mainly Standing, OBE and The Count and burst into a superb rendition of the old TRF favourite "Who ate all the pies? Who ate all the pies? Charlie Allan, You Fat Bastard, You ate all the pies".

The first half was spent with the TRF barber shop quartet going through their full rendition of obscure songs, most of them concerning hats for some strange reason, no doubt stemming from a Freudian hat fetish of Mainly Standing's. "Ay ay ay ay. Somebody Stole My Sombrero" got some particularly strange looks from the Rudolphs around us. Can't think why.

On the park the fare was less entertaining. Dunfermline threatened to get into the box on the odd occasion but Theo wasn't troubled. At the other end Van De Kamp made good saves from Dodds and Grant. Half-time arrived with the score 0-0 and all thoughts of Dunfermline making a game of it were surely extinguished.

Five minutes into the second half Billy Dodds provided us with a carbon copy of his winning goal against Hearts, a flick header from a Stephen Wright cross. 4-1 to the Aberdeen.

The party can now really begin, any lingering fears that Dunfermline might make a Lazarus-type comeback are gone. With Dunfermline at last committed to all out attack Joe Miller finally gets his first goal of the season, one that is fully deserved for his efforts over the closing weeks of the campaign. That Dunfermline manage to score goes almost unnoticed by the Red Army who are in full-scale celebration mode.

The icing on the comeback cake is provided by Stephen Glass, who waltzes round the Dunfermline defence, round Van De Kamp, who to be fair didn't attempt to haul him down, and strokes it into the empty net. His third goal in three games, a Pittodrie legend is being born before our eyes.

At full-time there is the inevitable pitch invasion, out of curiosity I decide to check out the playing surface to see how well it stood up to the ninety minutes, purely out of horticultural interest you understand. A few neds go to taunt the Dunfermline fans who, to their credit do not react. Mostly we go to salute the players who have dug us out of the deepest hole we've ever been in.

Of course the Glasgow press will fill out their match reports with tales of the Aberdeen hooligans who ruined the occasion. I seem to remember when the Huns dismantled Pittodrie in 1988 it was "joyous scenes from the Ibrox faithful", enough said.

It was all over, we'd saved the day, proved everyone wrong. The Bear had managed to get players that we knew were talented to believe it themselves. Billy Dodds, much maligned for his misses throughout the season had scored six goals in six games when the pressure was at its greatest. Joe Miller, a forgotten man under Willie Miller, had been a star in almost every game going down the stretch. The return of Brian Irvine had added passion the team. Peter Hetherston had put some guile and purpose into a pedestrian midfield. Duncan Shearer had proved there's no better finisher in the business and Stewart McKimmie had overcome his early season run-in with the fans to turn in his best performances in a Dons' shirt for three or four seasons.

But this was the same squad who got us into the mess in the first place so we shouldn't spend too much time thanking them for getting us back on the straight and narrow. The true stars were the fans who showed passion and support beyond the call of duty. The ovation given after the Kilmarnock game was the start of the road back. The enthusiasm inspired the club. Driven on by huge travelling supports and emotional home supports, the players responded and the press hated it. In his report after the Falkirk game Ewan Graham of The Hun gave our travelling support of 8,000 one out of ten for vocal support (season's average). Pure nastiness by a talentless hack who couldn't bear to see the Dons survive and the Rudolphs in full cry. Make yourself known next time you're in town Ewan, there's a few people would like a word in your Hun-loving shell-like.

We do not know what lies ahead. There must be changes in staff, players must be allowed to leave but must be replaced by quality. We cannot allow ourselves to fall into the same situation as last year when Rico left a void in the midfield that was not filled. We must continue to give the same support in every game as we did over the last half dozen this season. We start on the same points as everyone else, we've got a clean slate and must ensure that the lessons from season 1994/95 are learned and the warnings are heeded. Lest We Forget.

Never, Ever, Ever Again......

So, that's it then, our most traumatic season. A period of worry, anger, nerves and frustration. A time during which factions could have developed but didn't. This is the most positive element to emerge from the detritus of 1994/95.

We don't need ya, media

At various points - Fir Park in December, the Huns at home in

February, Fir Park again in April, Tynecastle, and the rest of the run-in and play offs - the united front shown by AFC management, players and fans sent a defiant message to those who wished us to fail. Let's not be coy about this. For all the noises that we heard from the media outside the city about the undesirability of the removal of the Dons from the Premier Division, the parasites were ready to rub their sweaty palms together in delight should we have failed. Let's not forget The Daily Record, Express, The Sun, the appalling Off The Ball, Scotsport, Sportscene and Bob Crampsey and Co.

How best to exact revenge? Well, stop buying their rags for starters. A sizeable hole in their North East circulation will hurt their Hun pockets most. The broadcasting media? Take every opportunity to use their phone-ins to wind them up and to put our point of view. We set Sparky, OBE, The Count and Mainly Standing out to put our views over and damn successful they have been too. Take your place under the camera gantry wherever we go and let them hear us. Make banners that stay on the correct side of libel and display them prominently....use your imagination, folks.....don't get mad, get even.

The Enema Within

Let's continue on the enemy meantime. There is an enemy within that needs to be dealt with. The 'put you downers' who seemingly cannot wait for a Dons' defeat to have a go at us at work or on the streets. Those for whom a Monday morning following a defeat is an opportunity to trot out the "Why do you waste your time?" crap to those of us who believe that time spent on the trail of the Reds at home or away is the best possible use of our allotted spans. Ignore them by all means, otherwise they've succeeded, but to really hack them off, refuse to give any help at all when tickets are in short supply for the big games when they'll turn up in a new scarf and matching golf umbrella. Remind them on such occasions that if you put your hand in the lion's cage, you will always be followed by the store detective in Woolies, Baghdad. Guaranteed to bring a pout to their thin-lipped gobs and an accusation of pettiness. Aye, right. Then tell them to piss off.

Closer to Home

In any inquest, fingers have to be pointed, so that learning can come from errors made. For us to have reached the pits as we did during 1994/95, some heinous mistakes must have been made.

The worst reaction would be to point fingers at individuals. In team situations-and everyone from fans to directors are the team-individual blaming and recrimination only destroys team spirit and sets individual against individual and faction against faction. Let's be content to observe that everyone from directors down has had some part to play in the blip that we hope 1994/95 turns out to be.

Mainly Standing has dealt copiously - no surprises there - with the Willie Miller situation earlier..er..doors in this volume. Everyone concerned with the real interests of AFC wanted him to be successful because he was, well....he was just Willie, our greatest ever player. As OBE said in his editorial in TRF 10, "...thanks for trying, loon...". Let's hope that recriminations don't last and that he can make his peace with the directors and be welcomed back as a fan, even wearing the Radio Scotland headset. We all saw, too late, and personally only after his departure, that he was not getting what was needed from a squadful of talent. Love is blind. So too, is Jim McCluskey.

Board Games

What of the Board? They have admitted to TRF representatives that errors were made, but they do appear desperate to turn things around. If Denis Miller, Gordon Buchan and Dave Johnston can convince the cynical hacks of TRF that the share issue (of which more below) is being offered to allow the club to put its future in the hands of the community, then it's likely that given the right medium and publicity, the local punters will be convinced too.

The Board's pledge to do more for the regular £10-at-the-gate fan will also be up for scrutiny. The fervour and goodwill for our club that was shown during the final few weeks of the season was obvious. The P&J series of "We're backing the Dons" personalities did not reflect the make up of the bulk of the paying clientele - it concentrated solely on the corporate customer, who like it or not, has become a part of the modern game. Let's ensure that you and I are in the queue when the goodwill starts flowing in the opposite direction.

Feed your ideas for improvement to PO Box 368. The directors have promised to keep the channel of communication open between themselves and the fans, both organised supporters clubs and the rabble that constitutes TRF. We'll make sure that the Board is kept informed of terrace Reds' thinking and we'll do what we can to keep them accountable to any promises they may make.

Playing With Fire (to avoid the drop)

No matter the managerial, coaching and administrative structure of the club, if the players are not achieving, then the whole edifice will fall around our ears. That nearly happened.

Again, pointing the finger at individuals will do nothing to improve the situation. All areas of the team, and nearly all individuals within those areas have been at fault at some times of the season. Certain players have been singled out for criticism. It's not big and it's not clever to barrack our own players as soon as they touch the ball. In one particular case, a player being criticised could not be faulted for lack of effort and his errors were all the more glaring because he refused to hide. Do you want Billy Stark back? The player in question knows himself that he is not Baggio, but where graft and effort towards the team cause is needed, I'd rather have him inside the tent pissing out than outside the tent pissing in......

It seems that Roy Aitken has instilled a bit of pride in the players again and we hope that he has the courage and receives the backing to complete the surgery and rebuilding that Willie Miller had to embark upon to sort out Smiffy's carnage. The appointment of our favourite slaphead (no, not Bloo Toon) to the post of Youth Development Manager may turn out to be one of the most important that has ever been made. If a half dozen or so Stephen Glasses are the result in the coming seasons, we'll all doff our sombreros to Aitken, Craig, Jarvie & Co.

I believe that the shock the club's managers received when the metaphorical jump leads were connected to the National Grid and hooked up to the collective AFC bollocks will be enough to ensure that Mr. Trauma will not be allowed to get beyond the Pittodrie bouncers again. Memories, however can be short, and if and when we taste success again, we must not allow complacency to sidle in as it appears to have done since the departure of Fergie and the loss of Chris Anderson. Eyes on the ball, everyone.

Bitching Back

Certain individuals, whose sole purpose in life seems to be to express bitterness at everything connected with AFC, will scoff at all this. They'll mutter "sell out" and "in the capitalist's pockets" and other such ill-informed tosh. Keep pinning up the Che Guevara posters lads, that'll change the world tomorrow.

Let's be honest. If we won the treble, the European Cup, the Derby, the Oaks, the Eurovision Song Contest, seven Oscars, found a cure for AIDS, eradicated cancer and heart disease, invented a supermarket trolley that travelled in a straight line, found a way of keeping Mainly Standing's imagination and genitular scribblings in check, discovered a chipper that made chips just like Violet's in Keith used to, piloted instant beer powder which guaranteed no hangover and won the General Election on a radical Socialist ticket, they'd still moan that a Pittodrie Pie costs 75p and that the meat content is 0.0006% below EC guidelines.

Fine. Despite the efforts of Government in the past sixteen years, we still allow a modicum of free speech. Carry on being part of the problem instead of part of the solution. That's your choice.

In the TRF Towers Library, among all the clutter that Sparky creates when he is rummaging through our back issues of "Skelp My Erse", we have several catalogues of lives. Come up and choose one sometime, you backbiting creeps. You know who you are. Still searching for the young asshole rebels? Some of us have developed a tiny bit and realise that there can be many ways of skinning a cat. (Please send details of your favoured method so that I can deal with the feline bastard who keeps shiting in my garden). Compromise is necessary sometimes, although this may offend the political purists. Give it some thought. We don't need the arrogance. Ta.

Heroes of the Struggle

On a more positive note, let's name the heroes. (It's a Goal) Duncan Shearer, Brian Irvine, Stephen Glass, Joe Miller and all the others

99

who played in the final few games with the verve, vigour, salt and vinegar which we all knew they had. Roy Aitken, too, for always believing and for maintaining the positive demeanour when we all thought we were down and out.

On the periphery, we salute John McRuvie for his rallying of the Red Army, both at Pittodrie and over the airwaves where he was aided, abetted and egged-on by Uncle Albert size-a-like Dave Macdermid and Andrew (Daley Thompson in negative) Shinie. More of the same please, and damn impartiality.

If the 4000 who were at Tynecastle, the 19500 who were at the United game, the 9000 at Brockville, the 19500 at the home play-off and the 8000 at the last game would care to send names to TRF, we'll give you all an individual namecheck in the Roll of Honour. You are the salt, pepper, mustard and vinegar of the good planet Earth. We love you all. Probably.

And finally friends and neighbours.......

So.....let's harness the goodwill and passion, Ian Donald. Let's give the heroes in the stands a proper say in the running of the club, for the good of us all and the sustainability of our main reason for existence. Put the shares on the market and watch them disappear. Be positive about it. No more talking the club and its stakeholders down. Make it meaningful and **do not ever think of taking our backing for granted.** That's been tried elsewhere and failed. We don't need the grief, thanks. Remember, the future belongs to those with the vision to see it. Provide it, convince us and we will follow, or lead if necessary.

Fellow Reds, dig deep for the share issue. It's an opportunity that will not come around again - grasp it.

The constancy of purpose shown by us all at the end of the season will have the Huns & Co quaking in their Predators if we keep it up. Remember how bad we felt after Stenhousemuir; then remember how good we felt as we raised the rafters and shocked the seagulls when we beat United. What better feeling is there? None. None at all.

Come on you Reds!